# THE WIRELESS STARS

by
George Nobbs

WENSUM BOOKS

WENSUM BOOKS (NORWICH) LTD.
33 Orford Place, Norwich NOR 06D.


First published November 1972

SBN 903 61900 8

Made and printed in Great Britain by
William Clowes & Sons Limited
London, Beccles and Colchester

# Contents

# Acknowledgements

I would like to record my grateful thanks to those individuals and organizations who have helped me in the preparation of this book. Clearly my task would have been impossible without the co-operation of the British Broadcasting Corporation. In particular, I would like to mention Mr R. D. Hewlett, Head of Reference and Registry Services, whose help and advice at all times was most welcome. I must also thank his staff and the staff of the following departments and sections: Sound Archives; Publicity and Photograph Library; B.B.C. Publications; the Written Archives Centre at Caversham; and the *Radio Times*.

A large number of people in the entertainment profession have given me advice and information and I would like to especially thank Mr Noël Johnson and Mr Donald Peers, both of whom spent a very considerable amount of time in answering my questions and checking the facts about the radio programmes with which they were associated. Their kindness and patience in assisting me is greatly appreciated.

A number of organizations and individuals have helped me with illustrations and information and I would like to thank *The Stage* for answering my many telephone inquiries and the staff of the *Daily Mirror*'s picture library in giving me access to their photograph collection at very short notice. The Keith Prowse Music Group and Decca Records both very kindly supplied material for illustrations.

I am grateful to the staff of Norwich Central Library and Norfolk County Library for obtaining a large number of books for my research. I would also like to thank Mr Malcolm Freegard of the Audio Visual Centre at the University of East Anglia for his help and advice, Mr Rodney Tompson for his photographic work and help with the layout of the book; Mr Tony Pratt for the original artwork which appears in the book; Mr Colin Baldwin for his cover design; Mr Kenneth Cooper for his excellent proof-reading; Barbara, Pat, and Dorothy for typing the manuscript, and Mr Peter Ward for the loan of illustrations.

Finally, I would like to acknowledge the following organizations for their permission to reproduce copyright illustrations: The British Broadcasting Corporation – pages 18, 24, 29, 37, 39, 41, 66, 68, 69, 74, 90, 92, 95, 118, 121, 124, 131, 132, 135, 136, 138, 149, 150, 151, 152, 154, 155. Radio Times Hulton Picture Library – pages 13, 16, 20, 27, 32, 33, 34, 36, 42, 46, 47, 49, 50, 54, 61, 64, 79, 80, 83, 117, 130, 137, 148. Syndication International Limited – pages 58, 70, 107, 109, 111, 123, 140. Keystone – pages 12, 45, 55, 57, 67, 82, 84, 112, 115, 116, 144, 153. Barratts – pages 11, 19, 21, 78, 142. Associated Newspapers Limited – pages 97, 112. *Radio Times* – page 114. Decca Records – page 113. Mr Peter Brough – page 128. Mr Noël Johnson – page 101.

George Nobbs

# Select Bibliography

BROUGH, PETER, *Educating Archie*, Stanley Paul & Co., 1955.
EDWARDS, JIMMY, *Take It From Me,* Werner Laurie, 1953.
HALL, HENRY, *Here's To The Next Time,* Odhams Press Ltd, 1955.
HANCOCK, FREDDIE & NATHAN, DAVID, *Hancock*, William Kimber, 1969.
HANDLEY, THOMAS, *Handley's Pages*, Stanley Paul and Co.
KAVANAGH, TED, *Tommy Handley*, Hodder & Stoughton, 1949.
MASCHWITZ, ERIC, *No Chip On My Shoulder*, Herbert Jenkins, 1957.
PAYNE, JACK, *Signature Tune*, Stanley Paul & Co.
PEERS, DONALD, *Pathway*, Werner Laurie, 1951.
PICKLES, WILFRED, *Between You And Me*, Werner Laurie, 1949.
PICKLES, WILFRED, *Sometime . . . Never*, Werner Laurie, 1951.
RAY, TED, *Raising The Laughs*, Werner Laurie, 1952.
RUMBOLD, GEOFFREY, *Here And There*, Vagabond Press.
WEBB, GEOFFREY, *The Inside Story Of Dick Barton*, Convoy Publications, 1950.
WORSLEY, FRANCIS, *Itma 1939–1948*, Vox Mundi Ltd., 1948.

ALLAN, ELKAN AND DORTHEAN, *Good Listening*, Hutchinson.
ANDREWS, CYRUS, *Radio And Television Who's Who*, George Young, 1954.
BRIGGS, ASA, *The History of Broadcasting In The United Kingdom,* Oxford University Press, Vol. 1, 1961; Vol. II, 1965; Vol. III, 1970.
BURTON, PAULU, *British Broadcasting: Radio And Television In The United Kingdom*, University of Minnesota Press, 1956.
COASE, R. H., *British Broadcasting, A Study In Monopoly*, Longman Green & Co., 1950.
ECKERSLEY, P. P., *The Power Behind The Microphone,* Cape, 1941.
MAINE, B. S., *The B.B.C. And Its Audience,* Nelson, 1939.

# 1. Birth of the B.B.C.

It is often forgotten that the now famous letters 'B.B.C.' were once the virtually unknown initials of a commercial company, composed of wireless manufacturers, which came into a precarious existence in 1922. By the end of that year it had a total staff of four people working from Magnet House, and an audience which consisted of enthusiasts for whom the actual 'receiving' of broadcasts was as exciting an achievement as their transmission.

When, in 1921, the Marconi Company had applied for permission to broadcast for half an hour a week the Post Office had doubted that the programmes would really be welcomed by amateurs, and had eventually agreed only to the transmission of calibration signals. Later during the year the Marconi Company broadcast a weekly half-hour from a hut at Writtle under the leadership of Peter Eckersley who acted, sang, played records, and chatted to the unseen audience. Already in America several fully fledged radio stations existed and broadcast concerts from The Hague could be received in this country.

Britain was falling behind in Wireless achievement, but by the summer of 1922 Writtle had been joined by another Marconi station – the legendary '2LO', and slowly but surely the permitted hours of broadcasting were extended. At the same time two other stations, owned by Anglo-American radio-manufacturing interests, opened up – one of which was the Manchester Metrovic station '2ZY'.

In the meantime, the Post Office had received a petition from representatives of sixty-three wireless societies expressing 'national resentment' about the fact that broadcasting was passing by default to foreign stations and that competent British companies who were willing to transmit weather reports, news, and music, were being refused permission to do so. By mid 1922 there was considerable pressure on the Government to make up its mind about its attitude to broadcasting and, slowly, the Post Office (which was to have no less than seven different Postmaster-Generals during the next three years) began negotiations with the leading radio interests. From the beginning the Government's idea was to avoid the responsibility of providing a broadcasting service of its own, but at the same time it had no wish to allow private-enterprise stations to proliferate as they had already done in America.

At first the general idea was that the various interested parties should operate separate stations rather on the pattern of the present system of allocating franchises to Commercial Television companies – the only difference being that with the wireless, the finance would be provided from licence revenue, not advertising. As time went by, however, the Postmaster-General began to encourage the individual companies to come to a general arrangement among themselves as to who should have stations and where. Negotiations went on for several months, chiefly because the 'Big Six' – manufacturing companies who had formed a sub-committee – were unable to reach agreement on who should construct the transmitting stations. The Marconi Company, who had virtually all the patents on the essential equipment, created difficulties and in the end the Post Office gave the go-ahead for two separate radio companies of which the B.B.C. was to be one. At the last minute, however, the Marconi Company relented and on the 18 October 1922 the British Broadcasting Company Limited was formed as the sole operator.

From the start wireless broadcasting was envisaged as a means of selling receiving sets, and the B.B.C. consisted entirely of British radio manufacturers. To them, the new company was seen as a necessary public obligation which had fallen upon them and as an encouragement to people buying receiving sets but never as a means of making a profit. Because of this situation it was possible for the B.B.C. to assume a public service attitude very early in its life, and when the time came to transform the organization into a public corporation there was little opposition from the manufacturing interests.

In the meantime, events began at last to move with some degree of speed. On 14 November 1922 the B.B.C. broadcast for the first time. As chance would have it it was also the day chosen for the General Election which ended the Coalition Government of David Lloyd George. On its very first day of existence the B.B.C. reported the Election results and the news that the Postmaster-General – Kellaway – had lost his seat. Kellaway, a former journalist turned politician, was assumed now to be the ideal man to take on the job of General Manager of the B.B.C., but to everybody's amazement, he promptly joined the Board of the Marconi Company. In December 1922, thirty-four-year-old ex-engineer John Reith accepted the post and began creating an institution in his own image.

When, in 1927, the British Broadcasting Company became a public corporation, 'The Wireless' had grown from a novelty to a near necessity. John Reith had quickly been promoted from General Manager to Managing Director of the Company, and now became Director-General of the new body. Under his leadership and with the skill and initiative of Peter Eckersley, the service had developed beyond recognition with the introduction of relay stations, the long-wave transmitter, alternative programmes, and probably most important of all, simultaneous broadcasting. By 'simultaneous' the B.B.C. meant what is today called 'networking'. Until 1924 each of the company's eight stations broadcast its own programmes, and it was only when Eckersley began experimenting with the G.P.O.'s national trunk-line telephone system, and the Western Electric Company's equipment that it was possible for one programme to be transmitted from several stations at the same time.

The various technical achievements of Peter Eckersley and his colleagues were to provide the B.B.C. with the means of giving a national service but there were many more difficulties with producing the subject-matter for the programmes. The newspapers didn't want the B.B.C. to broadcast news – at least not unless it was very old news – and the theatrical impresarios did everything they could, short of kidnapping, to prevent variety artists from broadcasting.

Probably the greatest achievement of the B.B.C. during its lifetime as a commercial concern was its part in the General Strike of 1926. It came very close to being taken over by those people who thought like Winston Churchill that the organization should be an arm of the Government. The fact that it survived was an indication of its strength, but the means which Reith and his staff were forced to employ in order to preserve their existence as an 'independent body' showed the weakness of the B.B.C.'s official position. Churchill did not manage to take it over, firstly, because Baldwin, the Prime Minister, didn't want him to – he had put Churchill in charge of the *British Gazette* and general propaganda in order to keep him out of mischief – and secondly, because the B.B.C. (or John Reith, which amounted to the same thing) was careful not to do anything which might offend or irritate the Government.

A form of voluntary censorship of features and talks was exercised, with Reith taking the responsibility and blame, but the news was, for the most part, delivered straight and the few incorrect items that slipped in were the results of error rather than policy. None the less, Reith deeply regretted having to refuse the strikers, and those who were sympathetic to them, the same facilities that the Company so readily extended to the Government.

By and large, however, the B.B.C. came out of the General Strike much stronger than it had gone in. Fleet Street had been closed down and the nation was at a virtual standstill, but the British Broadcasting Company kept on the air, and delivered news bulletins every hour. It did much to strengthen the prestige and authority of 'The Wireless', and it was none other than John Reith himself who read the news which announced the beginning of the General Strike. And by pure chance, it was he who happened to be on duty in the news studio when the news came that the strike was over.

The vast majority of the listening public were delighted with the service that the B.B.C. had provided, with everybody recognizing that it had been a significant factor in holding the country together during the crisis.

The prestige of 'The Wireless' was further enhanced in the brief pre-Corporation days by a variety of Royal broadcasters. King George V made history when he spoke on the radio at the British Empire Exhibition on St George's Day, 1924, and the Marconi Company had transmitted a speech by the Prince of Wales at a National Scout Rally in October 1922 (a month before the B.B.C. came into existence). By the year 1925, all the leading members of the Royal Family had been on the air.

The change from Company to Corporation was a smooth one; the shareholders were paid off by the Government and the Directors were replaced by Governors, but the transition was hardly noticed by B.B.C. staff or the listeners – indeed, announcers had often to be reminded not to continue to refer to the British Broadcasting *Company* after the change.

The twelve years that led to the outbreak of war in 1939 were rather a lean time for Light Entertainment. Sir John Reith (he had, after a lot of heart-searching, accepted a knighthood in 1926) had a distaste for variety shows, 'dance-band singers', and the like. To him the B.B.C. was a sacred trust and his mission was to educate and inform the British public and, of course, to make 'The Wireless' respectable. If the listeners were often bored to tears, it mattered little because the B.B.C. enjoyed a monopoly of broadcasting in Britain. But not, as became obvious in the early thirties, of broadcasting *to* Britain. When Radio Luxemburg and Radio Normandie began transmitting English-language Light Entertainment programmes to this country, it constituted the opening shots in a war between the advocates of State monopoly and of the supporters of commercial radio. It was to be a long war, and one which the B.B.C. would eventually lose completely, but in the 1930s that result was a long way off.

The lack of Light Entertainment of a high and regular standard was not entirely a result of Reith's personal convictions. The theatrical impresarios were also very much to blame. It was they who drew up contracts that prevented most variety stars from broadcasting (Ted Ray didn't appear on the air until 1939, because of contractual arrangements). But it wasn't only the theatrical managers and agents who would not co-operate. Many top-line variety stars just could not make the transition from the footlights to the microphone, or were afraid of broadcasting an act that had taken them years to put together and that had years of use still left in it.

The B.B.C. overcame these difficulties up to a point by recruiting their own artists and creating broadcasting stars. 'Our Lizzie' was one. She made her radio début three days after the B.B.C. first went on the air. ''Ullo! me old ducks, 'ere I am again with my old string bag', were her opening words, and she went on to sing 'Ours is a nice 'ouse ours is'. Our Lizzie was played by Helen Millais, and to her must go the honour of being the first comic character to be created by the Wireless. She was closely followed by John Henry, a Yorkshireman who related his tiffs with his wife Blossom and the exploits of his friend Joe Murgatroyd.

One of his earliest broadcasts was made in an aeroplane which Sir Alan Cobham piloted over London with John Henry and Blossom as passengers. The B.B.C. was quick to publicize its new star who became an overnight success enjoying the distinction of having roses named after him, and being recognized wherever he went. And Blossom's catch-phrase 'John Henry, come here!' was one of the first to capture the public's imagination.

Mabel Constanduros created the character of 'Mrs Buggins' when she made her first broadcast in 1925, and soon afterwards the B.B.C. informed her that they intended to make her one of its stars, which meant, in practical terms, that in future she would be paid five guineas per broadcast instead of the two she had received till now. The people who played Mrs Buggins, Our Lizzie and John Henry were among many who adapted themselves to the new medium. Willie Rouse, Wish Wynne, Robb Wilton, and Norman ('A smile, a song, and a piano') Long, were others who, by means of the Wireless, became 'Top of the Bill' attractions all over the country. A card was handed to each of them, as it was to all artists on their first broadcast, which read 'No gags on Scotsmen, Welshmen, Clergymen, Drink or Medical matters. Do not sneeze into the microphone'!

There was a sharp distinction between what the B.B.C. paid to its own 'house stars' (one guinea was quite usual) and the colossal sums (up to an exceptional sum of one thousand pounds for a single broadcast) that were given to outside 'big names' like Sir Harry Lauder, George Bernard Shaw, Noel Coward, Douglas Fairbanks senior, Mary Pickford, Tom Mix, and the Chocolate Coloured Coon – G. H. Elliot. It was felt that their prestige and publicity value warranted these amounts, but at the same time the B.B.C. denied publicity to a large group of broadcasters who the public wanted to hear about – the newsreaders and announcers.

After 1924 Reith decided that these hitherto well-known figures should become anonymous and that a standard form of announcing should prevail throughout the country. Excessive fear of the American style of broadcasting seemed to have dominated Reith's thinking at this time, and led to this ruling which, with few notable exceptions, remained in force until the war.

In 1928, however, the B.B.C. took a major

*Mr Jack Payne and his Hotel Orchestra, 1928.*

step towards the personality orientated programme when it engaged Mr Jack Payne as the Director of the B.B.C. Dance Orchestra. It was to be in fact an enlarged version of the orchestra that had previously played under his direction at the Hotel Cecil in London. All the musicians were paid by Payne himself, and the early *Radio Times* billing of 'The B.B.C. Dance Orchestra, personally conducted by Mr Jack Payne' was soon changed at his request to 'Jack Payne and his B.B.C. Dance Orchestra'. Payne, although an accomplished and successful dance-band leader in 1928, was *made* by the B.B.C. and he created a national sensation when, in 1932, he left the Corporation to go into 'show business'. This was the first major demonstration of the fact that broadcasting, even with its low fees, could turn a person into a 'Top of the Bill' attraction at any theatre

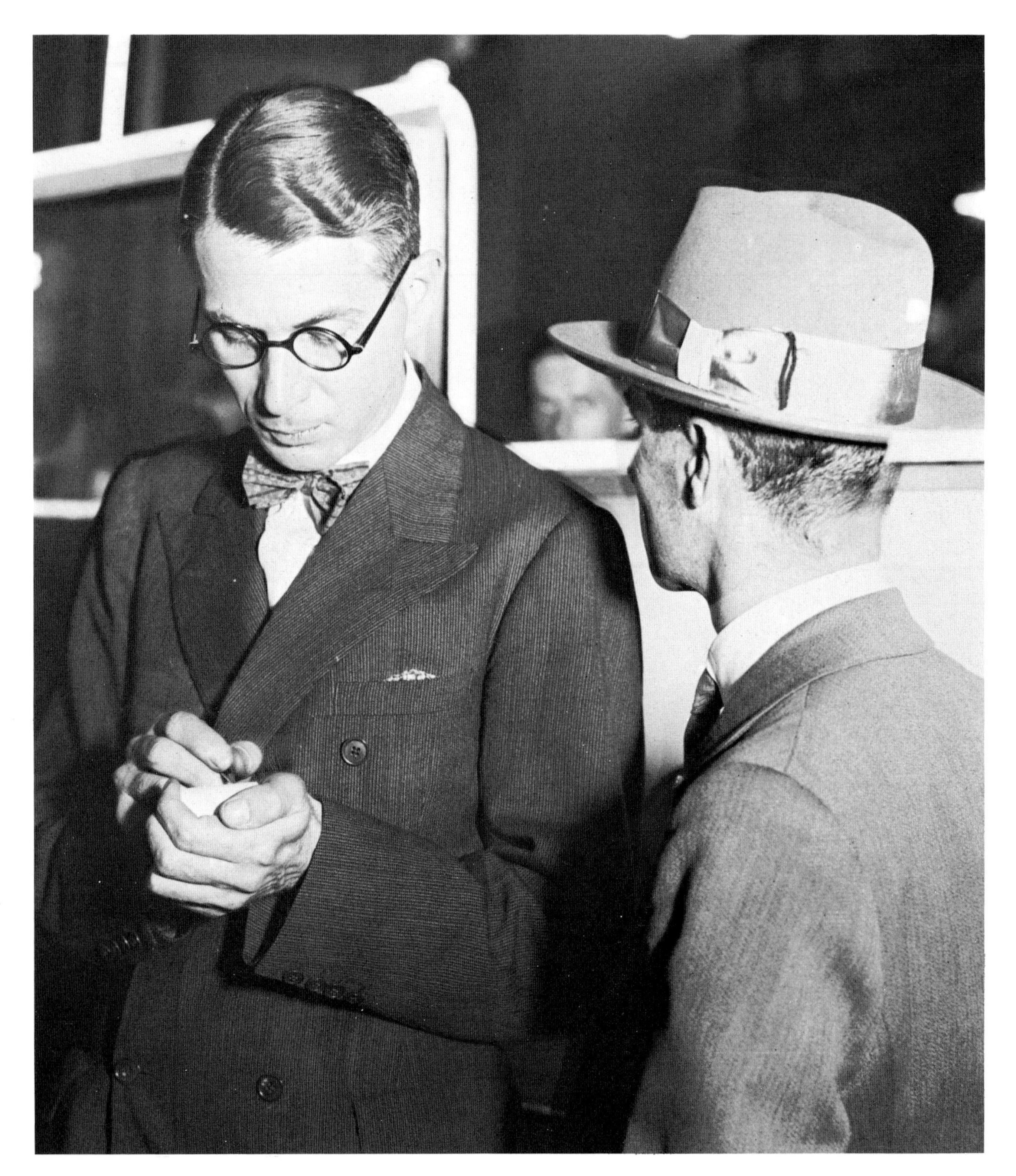

*Henry Hall signs an autograph.*

*Jack Payne and his Orchestra enter 'show business', 1932.*

in Britain and lead to the really big money.

As it was, the B.B.C. coped with the situation easily, and in the place of Mr Jack Payne's signature-tune 'Say it with Music', a new number, with lyrics by Roger Eckersley (the Assistant Controller of Programmes) and entitled 'Here's To The Next Time' introduced Henry Hall and his Orchestra on 15 March 1932. It was the first piece of music to be played from the newly completed Broadcasting House.

# IN TOWN TO-NIGHT
## (KNIGHTSBRIDGE)

*From the Suite*
**"LONDON"**

*By*
**ERIC COATES**

CHAPPELL & Co LTD.
50, NEW BOND STREET, LONDON, W. 1
NEW YORK SYDNEY
S.A.F. CHAPPELL,
86, BOULEVARD HAUSSMANN, PARIS.

PIANO SOLO
PRICE 2/- NET.

PRINTED IN ENGLAND.

# 2. Early Days

In 1933 the B.B.C., bowing to the inevitable, as Reith probably saw it, created a separate Variety Department headed by Eric Maschwitz, a former *Radio Times* editor. Maschwitz, who was married to Hermione Gingold, had already achieved fame by writing the very popular song 'These Foolish Things' and in 1932 had, with George Posford, written the musical *Good-night Vienna* for the B.B.C. (it was subsequently filmed by Herbert Wilcox and starred Jack Buchanan and Anna Neagle).

His appointment came in the aftermath of the opening stage of the battle with the continental commercial stations and of renewed difficulties from the Theatre-owners. A temporary and quite successful arrangement had been working with George Black of the General Theatre Corporation and Moss Empires, by which the B.B.C. relayed his Palladium show. In 1931, however, the B.B.C. decided to discontinue the practice for reasons of economy, whereupon Black reimposed a ban, which he had lifted in 1928, on his artists taking part in broadcasts. In 1933, having vainly searched for a compromise, the B.B.C. decided not to give any further fees, subsidies, or publicity to Black's companies; they would have to try and attract artists by the publicity value of broadcasting (they admitted that they were unable to offer a livelihood to variety stars) or fall back on record programmes and 'house artists'.

This new realistic policy at least gave the Variety Department a policy which they could follow and led to the introduction of a limited type of regular 'series' programmes – the term used by the B.B.C. was 'fixed points'. These had always existed in the form of The News, Religious Services, and *Children's Hour*. Now the practice was extended with great success to cover Variety with *In Town Tonight* as one of the first examples which Eric Maschwitz conceived as a 'shop window for any topical feature' that occurred too late to be included in the *Radio Times* – but then Maschwitz was a former editor of that journal. This idea of putting together surprise items and programme news that had previously been broadcast separately at random times, was immensely popular – as was the signature-tune, Eric Coates's 'Knightsbridge March'. A month after the first *In Town Tonight* went on the air, Leslie Bailey produced the first *Scrapbook* and in the same year the first serial thriller, *The Mystery of the Seven Cafés*, appeared.

Before 1933 there had been only three variety series in the B.B.C.'s history: John Watts's *Songs from the Shows* which began in April 1931, Ernest Longstaffe's *Music Hall* which commenced in March 1932, and Harry S. Pepper's *White Coons' Concert Party*, first heard at the end of that year. These programmes (they were joined in January 1933 by *The Kentucky Minstrels*) were all to enjoy long runs and encouraged Maschwitz to introduce more series. But now they were to be more the products of radio than relays of the studio variety shows that tended to give the impression that Broadcasting House was situated at the end of an Edwardian sea-side pier.

*Michael Standing interviewing people for* In Town Tonight.

Things had reached ludicrous proportions in 1932 when a full-time troupe of chorus-girls were engaged for studio shows 'to lend atmosphere'. The girls never sang and the sound of their dancing could have been better achieved by the Special Effects Department. Eventually they quietly disappeared, the casualties of the change that was taking place at the B.B.C. as it entered its second decade.

The B.B.C.'s more sophisticated attitude to Light Entertainment wasn't entirely voluntary – competition was beginning to become real by 1933 and it was coming from commercial stations, of all things! Many countries allowed sponsored programmes and occasionally attempts had been made to appeal to British listeners by broadcasting English-language items from foreign stations, but this had left the B.B.C. unperturbed; indeed, occasionally, these broadcasts had been advertised in the *Radio Times*. The situation changed in March 1930 when Captain Plugge (later M.P. for Chatham) registered the International Broadcasting Company, known as the 'I.B.C.'. Its object was to sell air-time to British advertisers on foreign stations and in October 1931 Radio Normandie, a ten-kilowatt station near Fécamp, began beaming I.B.C. programmes to a large audience in the South of England. The B.B.C. protested about the transmissions which they claimed had 'a blatant American manner' and asked the General Post Office to complain to the International Broadcasting Union. By spring 1933 Radio Normandie had been joined by Radio Luxemburg – a much more powerful station operating from the Grand Duchy with French finance, and the full approval of the Luxemburg Government.

The B.B.C.'s objections, which were to be heard again in the late 1960s, were very high-minded and unselfish. It was unfair, they said, for Luxemburg to use a wavelength that another country had once been offered (but had never used) and they went on to complain that commercial broadcasts endangered shipping messages and so on – the arguments are familiar. What was strange, however, was that the use of these wavelengths by Radio Normandie and Radio Luxemburg would immediately cease to congest the air-waves and endanger shipping if the advertisements were dropped and the programmes made less 'blatantly American'. Unfortunately for the B.B.C., the G.P.O. refused to ban the land-line relays of the commercial stations and the listening public soon became very attached to the 'pirates' (the B.B.C. was already using this term in the early 1930s) who captured half the British audience every Sunday.

The reason was not surprising. The B.B.C.'s Sunday programmes were designed to meet the Calvinistic standards of Lord Reith, while the commercial stations (unfairly, as the B.B.C. probably saw it) aimed to give entertainment to the British listeners. Radio Luxemburg relied very heavily on record programmes and Radio Normandie consistently produced a higher standard of wireless show.

Despite any efforts to the contrary, Radios Luxemburg and Normandie stayed on the air – a constant thorn in the side of the B.B.C. no doubt, but none the less a very popular service to the listeners. As the years progressed and the commercial stations prospered, the B.B.C.'s attitude changed; the objections became more plausible but at the same time the protagonists of sponsored radio, notably the Prime Minister of Luxemburg, the French Government and of course those British commercial interests who set the whole thing up, grew bolder. In the end, in 1939, the British Government was not only prepared to tolerate the 'pirates' but also, when war became imminent, anxious to keep the commercial stations running.

Indeed, Sir Robert Vansittart of the Foreign Office and Robert Boothby urged the Government to buy time on Radios Luxemburg and Normandie to advertise British war aims.

Perhaps the most poignant note was struck by Radio Luxemburg itself when it played, on its last transmission, an anthem composed by a Luxemburg citizen and entitled 'To Liberty'. The composition was sung in the Luxemburg language which none of the listeners, and very few of the inhabitants of the Grand Duchy, could understand. But by then it didn't really matter. The war that the commercial stations had fought against the B.B.C. had little relevance to the greater conflict which was being unleashed in Europe.

*Richard Murdoch and Arthur Askey in* Bandwagon, *1938.*

# 3. Bandwagon

The advent of commercial radio had, of course, had its effect on the B.B.C. And so had the influence of American broadcasting (Lord Reith had left the Corporation in 1938 and so American radio was no longer taboo). The first conscious effort of the B.B.C. to create a rival to the transatlantic and commercial programme was *Bandwagon*.

Before *Bandwagon* there had been a programme called *Monday Night at Seven* (later entitled *Monday Night at Eight*) which was the link between the old style of B.B.C. Light Entertainment and the thoroughly new approach which *Bandwagon* represented. *Monday Night at Eight* had one great advantage in its very title which summed up the whole argument for regular fixed-time programmes. The name gave it an identity as well as being in itself an advertisement for the show. It included 'Puzzle Corner' the first quiz ever to be directed to the listeners; a character called 'Mr Penny' who had a ten-minute adventure each week and, perhaps most memorable, 'Inspector Hornleigh' who investigated and solved crimes with the aid of the criminal's *one* mistake. The listeners heard this episode early in the programme and were given the answer as to just *what* the mistake was later in the show. It was a step forward but it was still in the old B.B.C. Variety tradition.

What was so different about *Bandwagon* was that it had a central character – in fact two characters – and it was a purely *radio* show. Its stars 'Big-Hearted' Arthur Askey and Dickie Murdoch took a lot of finding but when the B.B.C. finally got them together they found that they were on a winner. Everything about the show was planned with the object of attracting the maximum audience. And it did. *Bandwagon* became the biggest success that the B.B.C. had enjoyed to date.

Arthur Askey was not unknown to wireless listeners (he had compèred a variety show called *February Fill-Dyke* in February 1936) but his background was mainly music hall. *Bandwagon* made him the national star that he still is thirty-five years after the programme first went on the air. Dickie Murdoch came from a slightly different background – that of musical revue. A song and dance man and juvenile lead, he too became an overnight success as 'Stinker' Murdoch.

What sort of programme was *Bandwagon*? Well for a start it was new – at least to the B.B.C. of 1938. And it was slick and fast paced. It had a catchy little signature-tune and a tremendously lavish musical backing supplied by Mr Jack Hylton whose orchestra had four spots in the show.

In those days it was the practice to break up comedy shows with songs and features, a custom that persisted until the mid 1950s. *Bandwagon* had, besides its musical interludes, two such

*Syd Walker appearing in* In Town Tonight.

*Askey and Murdoch arriving for a recording in 1939.*

features in the form of 'Chestnut Corner' and 'Mr Walker Wants to Know'. And it had its catch-phrases – rather a novelty then but now an essential part of a comedy show. '*AYTHANG-YEW!*' or 'I thank you' made famous by 'Big-Hearted' Arthur Askey is still in use today although 'you silly little man' and 'proper um-drum' have not survived.

Perhaps the most important thing about it though was its 'radio-ness' for Askey and Murdoch's performance would have been meaningless on a stage. Their adventures invariably ended violently – like the time when Askey sat on a cinema organ which rose from the floor, as they usually did, but didn't stop and eventually crashed through the ceiling. It was the sort of Surrealist humour that was to reappear almost a generation later in television comedy but it was designed for the realm of radio where anything could happen – providing you had the right sound-effects. What was so good about *Bandwagon* was that its producers were realizing this fact for probably the first time.

Altogether, the show was amazingly sophisticated for 1938 and vastly superior to most television and radio comedy today. Many of the jokes that Askey and Murdoch related, to the accompaniment of groans, in 'Chestnut Corner' – a clever device for getting away with murder – still crop up as original humour in today's programmes. One feature of the show, however, was delightfully *un*sophisticated and that was 'Mr Walker Wants to Know'. Syd Walker who played an old Cockney junkman with an unlimited supply of homespun philosophy was very much a creature of his time. He was introduced by stirring music, rather reminiscent of the kind *Pathé News* used as background for Army manœuvres, and 'Yes, it's your old china Syd Walker still seeing it through chums' were the words that he used to introduce himself to his audience. Then he would relate an episode that had happened to him in the last week and invite his listeners to write in advising him on what action to take. 'What would you do chums?' – it became a catch-phrase used by millions of the homely philosopher's fans, and thousands did respond each week when he said 'Drop me a postcard and tell me what *you* would have done.'

Charming and popular as it was, the 'Mr Walker Wants to Know' feature was really totally irrelevant to the adventures of *Bandwagon*'s principals, Askey and Murdoch, who lived in 'the flat over the B.B.C.' surrounded by such seldom heard but much talked about characters as 'Mrs Bagwash', her daughter 'Nausea', and 'Lewis the Goat'.

So great was the success of the formula that in early 1939 the B.B.C. started looking around for another show of the same type. What was required was a two-part team, some comic supporting characters, and lots of catch-phrases. They found what they wanted and a new series went on the air on 12 July 1939. However, it wasn't a great success and the B.B.C. reflected that it didn't come near to the universal appeal of *Bandwagon* – 'perhaps the most popular radio show of all time'. The title of the new series, which the B.B.C. considered 'badly supported and ill-received', was *It's That Man Again*.

# 4. ITMA

Of all the shows in the history of British radio *ITMA* stands out as the one that most successfully made the variety show acceptable to the 'highbrow' audience. It was both an institution and a legend. With the death of Tommy Handley it was elevated even higher to become a sacred memory which even today remains inviolate. Which is all rather silly really because *ITMA* was *just* a comedy show despite the many efforts that have been made to read something else into it. Its star Tommy Handley, its producer Francis Worsley, and its writer Ted Kavanagh had but one object – to make the audience laugh. And in this they eventually succeeded more brilliantly than anybody had done before. But the humour was based on puns, catch-phrases, topical gags, sound-effects, and comic characters with Dickensian names. It was not a programme with a message or 'something to say' – it was pure fun and those who treat its memory too reverently and intellectually do it a disservice.

It was conceived as a British version of *The Burns and Allen Show*. That in itself is sufficient to make *ITMA* both significant and amusing. Of course it turned out to be nothing like its one-time American model because Tommy Handley, its star, was a totally different type of performer to George Burns who was essentially the straight man or 'feed' of the Burns and Allen team. Handley on the other hand was a fast-talking comic who had been broadcasting with great success since 1924 although he had never appeared in a radio *series*. He was teamed-up, for the new show, with a Canadian girl called Celia Eddy but it was quite obvious that the Burns and Allen formula wouldn't work with its 'feed–comic' relationship reversed.

Several scripts were prepared but none were considered suitable and Handley suggested to producer Francis Worsley that an old friend, Ted Kavanagh, should be called in. An hour later the three met in the old Langham Hotel which stands opposite Broadcasting House, and is now part of the B.B.C. Worsley recalled that they had three pink gins, although Kavanagh remembered three very large lagers, but both agreed that the hotel was packed out with clergymen attending a conference. There amid an Anglican Tower of Babel the three worked out a formula for the show.

They came up with the idea of setting the series on board a ship, 'a sort of Mad Hatter's "Strength Through Joy" cruising vessel' according to Kavanagh. It is indeed typical of *ITMA*, where nearly every joke was topical, that even this description needs an explanation – 'Strength Through Joy' was of course the slogan of the Nazi's German Labour Front. Worsley in his book *ITMA 1939–1948* described it as a floating broadcasting ship where Handley could send out 'ridiculous programmes of his own concoction'.

Celia Eddy was cast as Handley's 'dumb blonde' secretary Cilly and Eric Egan played a mad Russian inventor called Vladivostooge whose presence as one of the ship's passengers was never explained.

It was still felt necessary to break up a comedy

*Tommy Handley.*

show with features and so two were included in the shape of 'Guess or No' in which Lionel Gamlin conducted a charade using play-titles, and 'Man Bites Dog' by Sam Heppner. Here everyday situations were reversed – for example a man looking for a job would interview his prospective employer. Pat Taylor was engaged as the show's singer and the London Casino supplied the band of Jack Harris. The title had been decided long ago.

It had been the *Daily Express* which had first turned the expression 'It's That Man Again' into a popular catch-phrase – it existed long before *ITMA* and referred not to Handley but to another fast-talking performer and radio personality, Adolf Hitler. Whenever the Führer discovered another 'intolerable burden' that the German Reich could no longer permit to continue, the *Daily Express* ran the phrase as a headline. The actual form of the title existed for only four episodes of the first series which was interrupted by the outbreak of war. When the programme returned to the air it used only those now-famous initials ITMA – this innovation, like so many others, was the suggestion of Tommy Handley. And *ITMA*, as became obvious ten years later when he died, was Tommy Handley.

Thomas Handley was born in Threlfall Street, Liverpool, in 1894. His father, a dairy-farmer, died when Tommy was still a baby and the future comedian was brought up by his mother. As soon as he was able to, young Handley started spending his pocket-money on disguises and he made up his mind that he was going to go 'on the stage'. His early attempts were mainly confined to Band of Hope concerts and amateur dramatic societies and it was only when he joined the Army in November 1917 that young Handley really became a professional entertainer. At first he was classified as 'Singer, baritone, light songs, of', but following a variety of amusing mishaps his status was soon changed to that of comic.

After a year in an Army concert party that also included G. H. Elliot, Handley was demobbed and out of work. During the previous twelve months he had taken part in almost a thousand shows given to a variety of audiences, including munition workers, dockers, stockbrokers, and the public at street corners. It had been a crash-course in show business but the problem now was to find work. A friend told him about auditions that were being held for a touring musical comedy called *Shanghai* and Tommy was engaged for a chorus part. Just to keep another friend company, he also auditioned for the D'Oyly Carte organization on the same day. Later in the week he was contacted by them and asked to join their No. 2 Gilbert and Sullivan Company but he had already signed up for the provincial tour of *Shanghai.*

It was in *Shanghai* that Tommy met Jack Hylton who was Musical Director of the show and when the tour finished Hylton managed to find Handley more work in a concert party he was involved in. For a time they even became a double act appearing at Lyons Popular Café in Piccadilly – although their partnership was short-lived the friendship with Hylton lasted for the rest of Handley's life and they were to frequently work together.

It was while appearing in a 'fit-up' show that Tommy was introduced to a sketch which he was to use as his stage act, off and on, from 1921 to 1941. It was called 'The Disorderly Room' and consisted of a mock court martial with all the speeches fitted to the music of popular songs of the day. At first Tommy was unimpressed by the sketch but soon changed his mind and during the next twenty years he must have played it to every music-hall audience in the country. It was in fact the act that he used in his very first broadcast – a relay of the Royal Command Performance of 1924.

Soon after that relay he was invited by a friend to audition for the B.B.C. – it was evidence of Handley's real popularity in the profession that friendly contacts played such a large part in his career. The idea of the audition was for Tommy to sing and then 'be funny'. He obliged with a song but when he had finished all his prepared patter vanished. He could think of nothing to say except 'Thirty days hath September, April, June and November' and then he forgot how it continued. He repeated the line again and then added in an embarrassed desperation, 'I can't remember the rest – go and work it out for yourselves.'

In the true Hollywood version of show-business tradition, Tommy was about to make a hurried and dejected exit when the producer came in overcome by laughter. It would be nice to say 'and the rest is radio history', but in fact it was to be fifteen years before Handley got a radio *series* and came into his own. The intervening years saw his marriage to singer Jean Allistone whom he met at Savoy Hill – it was the first 'radio romance'. They worked together in several early programmes and Tommy continued touring the Halls with 'The Disorderly Room'. He also became involved in film work, making several comedies himself and supplying the commentaries to a series of reissued Chaplin 'silents'. But it was on the air that Tommy was making his name, in a variety of solo programmes, as a good wireless comic. His work ranged from *Children's Hour* to the *White Coons' Concert Party* and included an exclusively radio act with Ronald Frankau called 'Murgatroyd and Winterbottom'.

So it was that when *Bandwagon* became a great national hit, Tommy Handley was chosen to repeat Arthur Askey's success and to star in his own series.

At 8.15 p.m. on Wednesday, 12 July 1939 an announcer said 'This is the National Programme – Ladies and Gentlemen – It's That Man Again', and that famous signature-tune was heard for the first time. Handley's opening words were spoken on the telephone, and went like this, 'Hello, is that Turner, Turner and Turtle? It is? Then good morning, good morning, good morning, good morning. It's that man again. That's right, Tommy Handley!'

By general consent the first show was a flop and the next three made little impression. The series was interrupted by Radiolympia and scheduled to return on 5 September but by then, of course, war had broken out and the B.B.C. Variety Department was evacuated to Bristol. Overnight, it seemed, huge Government departments had sprung up, known by ominous initials although in fact they, like the B.B.C.'s evacuation plans, had been prepared long ago. It was decided that the show should exploit the humorous side of this by appointing Tommy as 'Minister of Aggravation and Mysteries' and that he should be housed in the 'Office of Twerps'. But these titles didn't provide easy-to-remember initials.

The problem seemed insoluble and while producer, writer, and star pondered over the next script, Tommy doodled with the show's title, blocking in the capitals of each word. It only needed saying once and *ITMA* appeared obvious, and the first show under that title went on the air on 19 September 1939. Its audience was huge because theatres and cinemas had been temporarily closed and the black-out had only just been introduced. So there was little to do except listen to the wireless. But despite these advantages it was to be another two years before *ITMA* came into its own.

Undoubtedly the great success, and real star,

of that first series was Funf, played by Jack Train.

He made his first appearance in the second *ITMA* programme on 26 September and he spoke, of course, on the telephone. 'Who's speaking?' asked Tommy. 'It is Funf, your favourite spy – I have found out everything', Jack replied. 'Do not leave your office – your life is in danger. Beware – you have enemies whom you do not know.'

In a blacked-out Britain, armed with gasmasks and led to expect total destruction of their cities by air at any moment, Funf was a means of relieving tension and overnight he became a national comic scapegoat. Jack Train also played Fusspot, a caricature of a civil servant whose catch-phrase was 'It's most irregular', and later he would become Colonel Chinstrap. Maurice Denham supplied the voice of Lola Tickle who told 'Mr ITMA' that she 'always did her best for all her gentlemen' and when, after the third programme, it was decided to replace the 'Guess or No' feature, Denham was heard again – this time as the announcer on ITMA's 'commercial station' Radio Fakenberg with Sam Costa singing

*Tommy Handley, Jack Train, and Ted Kavanagh at Bangor.*

the 'commercial'.

The first series ended on a high note and although it still trailed behind *Bandwagon* in popularity, it had laid the foundations of its future success. When it returned to the air in June 1941 the B.B.C. Variety Department had moved from Bristol to Bangor and the locale of *ITMA* was also moved – to the imaginary resort of Foaming-at-the-Mouth. Here Tommy Handley was to be elected Mayor and to administer the town with the aid of a host of new characters.

'Boss, Boss, sumpin' terrible's happened!' was the catch-phrase of the Mayor's American henchman and election agent Sam Scram (played by Sidney Keith) while Horace Percival provided the voice of Ali Oop who was always either trying to sell Tommy postcards or obtain a licence to peddle 'ice-cream, bootlaces, Persian carpets, trays on the beach'. Percival also played The Diver. This character was based on someone from Tommy's own childhood holidays at New Brighton. 'Don't forget the diver, sir; don't forget the diver' had been the actual words used by a figure in bathing-suit who held out a butterfly-net to the ferryboat trippers in those far-off days. Tommy recalled that he never saw him as much as put his foot in the water. His other catch-phrase, 'I'm going down now, sir' was universally adopted by everybody from fighter pilots to lift attendants. And then there were Claude and Cecil (Jack Train and Horace Percival) with their 'After *you* Claude!' 'No, after *you* Cecil', and Lefty (Sam Scram's friend) who always failed to carry out his threat to 'bump off' Tommy with the explanation 'It's me noives.'

Hari Kari, the Japanese Sandman, appeared in the fourth programme of this series and, like Funf, conducted all his conversations on the telephone. Only Tommy could understand what Hari Kari was saying and replied with such phrases as 'You'll find it on the end of the pier', or 'I know it's open, I went there myself yesterday.' The series ended with a peace overture from Funf (Hess had flown to Britain on his own initiative, a few weeks earlier) – 'All I have said back I will take. All I have done I will undo. Your buddy I want to be. Peace we will make. Meet me at the lighthouse at 8.45 tonight – double-crossing time', said Funf's letter. Anyway, Tommy went with his henchmen but although the Mayor claimed to see Funf through the keyhole he managed to elude capture.

This series had been entitled *ITSA*, which stood for 'It's That Sand Again' – and it had been remarkably short, starting in June and ending in July 1941 but it did mark the turn of the tide for *ITMA* which returned for a third series on 25 September 1941.

This new series was to establish *ITMA* as the B.B.C.'s most listened to variety show to date – a title previously enjoyed by *Bandwagon*.

The extraneous 'features' like 'Guess or No' had been dropped in the previous series and now the show consisted entirely of Tommy coping with interruptions from his many existing friends and the new ones who made their appearance in the succeeding programmes.

As soon as Tommy alighted from the train which brought him back to Foaming-at-the-Mouth, he was able to introduce his foreign secretary Signor So-So (played by Milan-born Dino Galvani). Now all three Axis Powers had accredited representatives at *ITMA*'s sea-side resort. But So-So was a different character to Funf and Hari Kari. He clearly worshipped the Mayor whom he referred to as 'Signor Handlebar' or 'Meestair Handpump' and he immediately endeared himself to the listeners.

Meanwhile, Clarence Wright created the cheery commercial traveller who popped up selling all

*Dorothy Summers (Mrs Mopp) and Tommy Handley.*

manner of products and said 'Good morning, *nice* day' at every opportunity. And then on 10 October 1941, to the accompaniment of a clattering bucket and brush, Dorothy Summers as Mrs Mopp asked 'Can I do for you now, Sir?' – later the word 'for' was dropped and the modified 'Can I do you now, Sir?' became perhaps *ITMA*'s best-remembered catch-phrase.

In the same series Colonel Chinstrap (Jack Train) appeared and denied that Tommy had met him in Rumbellipore. 'You did not, Sir. I was never there!' 'Then you must have a double!' exclaimed Tommy to which the Colonel replied 'Thanks I will.' Most Handley–Chinstrap conversations took this form although later the last line became 'I don't mind if I do.'

From now on new characters appeared thick and fast and so did their catch-phrases. Mrs Mopp had introduced 'T.T.F.N.' ('Ta ta for now') and 'I brought this for you, Sir!' Ali Oop said 'I go, I come back', and Norman the Doorman (Fred Yule) always said 'Vicky Verky.' And then there

was 'the Man from the Ministry' played by Clarence Wright, who repeated the last phrase of every sentence – 'I've come to inspect your factory, I said inspect your factory.'

Many of them had Dickensian names that indicated their occupations or attitudes; there was Luke Smart the tailor, Bookham the variety agent, Pansy Cowe-Parsley the fresh-air fiend and nature-lover, and Percy Pintable ('Lo and be'old' he always said). He had a daughter called Effie who introduced herself as 'seventeen and never been out with an American'.

And then there was Mr What's'isname (played by Horace Percival) who could never complete a sentence, and Comical Chris (Bill Stephens) who was forever resurrecting old jokes. Walter Wetwhite did imitations and another Percival character always came up with conundrums.

Funf introduced his jovial practical-joking friend Johann Bull (Fred Yule) and Sam Scram invited his brother Butch over from the States. Everybody in the show, except Handley, knew a mysterious Scot called Peter Geekie but although he always cropped up in conversation he never

*An* ITMA *script conference.*

*Dorothy Summers and Tommy Handley in a 1942 edition of* ITMA.

put in an appearance.

And there was the ebullient Marquis of Mourne, Dr Smack the headmaster, Tommy's Aunt Sally, and an ancient character called Mark Time who often replied 'I'll have to ask me Dad.'

These, together with Tommy's faithful secretary Miss Hotchkiss, were the war-time characters of *ITMA*. By 1945 they had left Foaming-at-the-Mouth and Tommy had in quick succession been factory manager, Squire of Much Fiddling, farmer, schoolteacher, hotel-owner and planner – the end of the war saw him as a Parliamentary candidate. Funf had all but disappeared but Signor So-So, the man originally entrusted with Mayor Handley's Twelve Week Plan, was still a firm favourite. Now with peace breaking out everywhere it was decided to drop many of the old characters and to make a radical change of locale. But the story of post-war *ITMA* belongs to a later chapter.

*Robb Wilton.*

# 5. The Day War Broke Out

'The day War Broke Out, my missus looked at me and said, "What good are you?" I said "Who?" She said "You." I said "How do you mean, what good am I?" She said "Well you're too old for the Army, you couldn't get into the Navy, and they wouldn't have you in the Air Force, so what good are you?" I said "How do I know – I'll have to think."'

There can be few people who can remember the war without recalling Robb Wilton and 'The day War Broke Out'. As Mr Muddlecombe, Wilton in his own full-length shows became a top radio star although he, like Handley, had been broadcasting since the B.B.C.'s pre-Corporation days. He was a symbol of war-time Britain but his radio style differed greatly from that of Churchill or Vera Lynn – to name but two other symbolic war-time broadcasters. Wilton was always rather confused and made gentle fun of the Home Guard long before *Dad's Army* was ever dreamt of, as this extract from one of his programmes shows:

'The first day I got my uniform I went home and put it on. The Missus looked at me and said "What are you supposed to be?" I said "Supposed to be? I'm one of the Home Guards." She said "One of the Home Guards? What are the others like?" She said "What are you supposed to do?" I said "I'm supposed to stop Hitler's Army landing!" She said "What *you*?" I said "No, not me, there's Bob Edwards, Charlie Evans, Billy Brightside – there's seven or eight of us, we're in a group on guard in a little hut behind The Dog and Pullet!"'

That was Wilton's style. Wilfred Pickles, discussing humour in his book *Sometime . . . Never*, said this about him: 'It is even harder to take Robb Wilton's fun to pieces for serious analysis. Yet the inimitable Robb had the nation roaring with laughter during those years of desperate anxiety and peril. Who will ever forget the cautiously protesting henpecked voice plaintively coming out of the loudspeaker with those memorable words that sum up an unforgettable milestone in the lives of most of us.' Pickles was referring to Wilton's Home Guard sketch. Ted Ray also paid tribute to him as someone whose work was 'pure comedy in every sense of the word, based on warm undertanding and love for humanity'.

Robb Wilton was one of several broadcasters whom the listeners took to their hearts during the war although Wilton probably enjoyed a greater degree of real affection than any other wireless star, with the exception of Tommy Handley. Actually, 'The day War Broke Out' found the B.B.C. much more prepared than the bewildered Robb. Months before plans had been made to evacuate the various Departments to Regional centres and staff were told that when the B.B.C. announcer said 'This is London' instead of 'This is the National Programme' they were to make their own way to their allotted destinations.

The Regional Service and the National Pro-

*Robb Wilton, Doreen Season, and Max Kester at Bangor.*

gramme were 'synchronized' as the B.B.C. put it – in fact they were replaced by a single programme which for the first few weeks of the war consisted almost entirely of news, records, and Sandy Macpherson at the B.B.C. Theatre Organ. By the end of 1939, however, the B.B.C. Variety Department rallied and began to provide the kind of service which was to be remembered so affectionately by listeners in later years. Following the uproar with which the Press and public had greeted the initial war-time service, the B.B.C. now decided to concentrate on variety between the hours of 6 p.m. and midnight with one major show and at least two subsidiary ones each night. *Monday Night at Eight* naturally led off the week followed by *ITMA* on Tuesday and Robb Wilton's *Mr Muddlecombe* on Wednesday. Thursday saw the return of *Henry Hall's Guest Night* and *Songs from the Shows* and although Friday night seemed at first to provide no major draw, Saturday ended up the week with both *Bandwagon* and *Garrison Theatre*.

*Jack Warner and Joan Winters in* Garrison Theatre, *1940*.

*Garrison Theatre* although popular enough was never a very distinguished programme. Most writers and historians of war-time broadcasting prefer to gloss over it and it is not difficult to see why. It was a show within a show, being based on the actual Northern Command Garrison Theatre of the First World War, as remembered by the programme's originators, Harry S. Pepper and Charles Shadwell, and consisted of a 'regular audience' of set characters. These were an irascible R.S.M., a soldier, and his girl-friend. But the soldier was played by Jack Warner and he had a catch-phrase, which was soon on everybody's lips – 'Mind my bike.' Warner as the soldier-compère managed to carry *Garrison Theatre* along the precarious heights of popularity and one can reflect with some justification that he has done the same thing, with the aid of a single catch-phrase – 'Evening All' – for *Dixon of Dock Green* for even longer.

Another new show which appeared in the early part of the war was *Hi Gang*, broadcast for the first time in May 1940. Its principals were all Americans but they were well known to British listeners. Ben Lyon and Bebe Daniels were both film stars in their own right and had been in Britain since 1936. Vic Oliver needed little introduction either, as he was married to Sarah Churchill the daughter of the Prime Minister.

The story of Ben and Bebe was a rather romantic one. Bebe Daniels was born in Texas. Her mother's family were Spanish-Americans and her father was Scottish. Both parents were in show business and Bebe made her first stage appearance at the age of four as the infant Duke of York in *Richard III*. When at the age of seven the Child Labour Laws put a stop to her work on stage, Bebe went into films and worked her way through an incredible series of short pictures – one a week for three and a half years. Her friends were Charlie Chaplin, William S. Hart, Mary Pickford, Douglas Fairbanks, and Rudolph Valentino, whom she starred with in *Monsieur Beaucaire*. But it was the film *Rio Rita* that made her into a really big star.

Ben Lyon, born in Atlanta, Georgia, had a passion for acting even as a small boy. Later his family moved to New York and it was there that Ben entered the film business. One day as he was walking to school he passed a studio and decided to go in. He noticed a rather impressive-looking individual on the set and asked him, 'How could I go about breaking into the movies mister?' 'Report here tomorrow,' came the reply – young Lyon had been speaking to the director.

Ben's most famous picture was *Hell's Angels* – made originally by Howard Hughes as a silent film. When it was completed Hughes decided to remake it as a talkie, keeping the same cast with the exception of Greta Nissen whose pronounced Swedish accent made her unsuitable for talking pictures.

It was Ben who solved this recasting problem when he spotted a young extra on the set and asked her to make a 'test' for the lead in *Hell's Angels*. At first she thought he was joking but eventually she agreed. Her name was Jean Harlow and *Hell's Angels* made a star of both she and Ben Lyon.

Ben married Bebe Daniels in 1930 and they first visited England in 1933. They came back in 1936 to do a music-hall tour in which they were billed as 'Hollywood's Happiest Married Couple' and it was a very accurate description. Apart from brief visits to the U.S.A. Ben and Bebe remained in England and, in 1939, after taking their two children to America, they returned to London to carry on their own private war against Hitler.

The third member of 'the Gang', Vic Oliver, was born in Vienna in 1898, the son of Baron Victor von Samek and Josephine Rauch. He studied music at the Vienna Conservatoire and became Assistant Conductor at the Graz Opera House. It was when he emigrated to America in 1922 that Vic relinquished his father's title and for several years he toured the U.S.A. as a concert violinist. Towards the end of the 1920s he became a comedian and it was in this role that he appeared at the Adelphi, London, in C. B. Cochran's *Follow the Sun* in 1936. Sarah Churchill was making her début in the chorus and later in the same year she and Vic Oliver were married in America. Like the Lyons, Vic had been resident in England since 1936 and in

Hi Gang. *Standing: Jay Wilbur, Sam Browne, Harry Pepper. Seated: Vic Oliver, Bebe Daniels, and Ben Lyon.*

May 1940 Ben, Bebe, and Vic made their first broadcast together in *Hi Gang*.

Like all products of American entertainment – and *Hi Gang was* mostly American even though it was produced by the B.B.C. – the appeal of the show was in its presentation rather than its basic content. It was introduced by a fanfare and, for some reason, had 'I'm Just Wild About Harry' as its signature-tune. Ben Lyon opened the show by shouting 'Hi Gang' and the audience roared the greeting back. From there on the show moved at a feverish pace; with fast patter broken up by well-orchestrated, well-played, and well-sung numbers. In a typical programme the songs included were 'Save a Little Sunshine', 'Happy Days Are Here Again' (this served as Vic's signature-tune), 'I've Got Rhythm', 'The Breeze and I' (sung by Bebe), and 'Just One More Chance'. The orchestra was that of Jay Wilbur and the singers were The Green Sisters and Sam Browne. Most of the dialogue consisted of light-hearted banter between the trio of Ben, Bebe, and Vic which they laced with the kind of friendly insults practised by Hope and Crosby.

Ben, as the compère, managed to race through the show until it was time to shout 'So Long Gang', receive the ritual reply and play the programme out with another frantic arrangement of 'I'm Just Wild About Harry'. The show's lack of brilliant material was more than made up for by this ability of Ben's to keep things going at a cracking pace. The polished style of the stars and the quick musical numbers were altogether new to British radio and the studio audience was clearly ecstatic. One wonders what Lord Reith thought about it. His abhorrence of things that were 'blatantly American' was well known – but he had left the B.B.C. in 1938. Before the end of the war the B.B.C. would be broadcasting imported American programmes and British comedians would become more like their American models, but *Hi Gang* was only one step in a journey that had been made inevitable by the success of *Bandwagon* and the needs of war.

*The Kentucky Minstrels* were still going strong in 1940, with Scott and Whaley – or Cuthbert and Pussyfoot – carrying on their quarrel which usually ended with both of them losing their place in the script. The show had hardly altered since it began, way back in January 1933, and the cast had remained almost the same too. Ike (Yow-sah) Hatch kept the modern rhythmic end of the show going while Doris Arnold supplied her arrangements of songs like 'The Lost Chord', 'The Holy City', and 'Abide With Me', all three of which became classics in radio history.

Denny Warren (Mr Bones) completed the list of the *Minstrels*' stars. His onslaught in his stump speeches on wives in general and his own in particular called forth protests from a large number of listeners who thought he actually meant what he said.

One of the heroes of war-time broadcasting was Sandy Macpherson who virtually single-handed kept the B.B.C. on the air in the early months of the war. He was born in Paris – which is a small town near Toronto in Canada – in 1897 and his real name was Roderick Hale Macpherson. During the First World War he served in the Canadian Forces and joined Metro-Goldwyn-Mayer in 1919. After touring North America he arrived in England in 1928 and became the organist at the Empire Cinema, Leicester Square. It was the *era* of the cinema organist, when the instrument would majestically rise from the floor in a galaxy of coloured lights and the organist would slowly turn, still playing, and smile at the audience.

In 1938 Sandy took over the most coveted

*Sandy Macpherson.*

organist's seat in the country when he succeeded Reginald Foort at the B.B.C. Theatre Organ. And so it was that a year later he was able to hold the fort for the B.B.C. during the trying early dislocations of war-time broadcasting.

Another person who did sterling work in keeping the airwaves occupied in those days was veteran disc jockey, Christopher Stone. Unlike Macpherson, Stone, who had created the profession of D.J. as long ago as 1927, was well known to listeners and his face appeared in endorsements of Bush radios in the *Radio Times* every week through three decades. With the special demands of war-time, there was a great increase in the Variety Department's output, which meant plenty of work for existing stars and opportunities for new ones. Established shows such as *The Kentucky Minstrels* flourished

*Christopher Stone.*

alongside innovations like *Hi Gang*; Christopher Stone could happily share the 'pop' scene with Sandy Macpherson; and Henry Hall could be as much a symbol of the war years as Vera Lynn.

*Henry Hall in a 'still' from his film* Music Hath Charms.

# 6. Here's to the Next Time

*Henry Hall's Guest Night* had returned to the air in December 1939. Hall, as you may recall, had replaced Jack Payne when the latter went into show business in 1932.

The future band-leader was born in London in 1898, the son of a blacksmith who later became a greengrocer. Both his parents were in the Salvation Army and it was their ambition that young Henry should play in the local Salvation Army band. The idea didn't appeal to him though, and as he says in his autobiography *Here's To The Next Time*, 'I was no infant prodigy, no Mozart creeping downstairs in my nightshirt to compose sonatas. I was just plain Harry Hall, the grocer's son, who had a bit of an ear for music.'

On leaving school he worked as a page boy in the National Health Insurance Commission and was very impressed by his employers. 'They were important people, yes; they were intelligent and had great business acumen; they had charm and social presence, but to me first and foremost, they were vital and exciting.' Young Henry made up his mind that he would be like them. Contact with them, he said, instilled in him a desire to make his name, to own a fine car, smoke cigars, and stay at the Savoy Hotel as they did.

His next job was in the Music Department of the Salvation Army and it consisted mainly of typing letters, proof-reading manuscript music, and copying out musical scores. And he wrote marches for 'the Army' in his spare time. The experience proved invaluable to young Henry – still in his early teens – and he recalled later that he was glad to have done his 'basic training' with the Salvation Army rather than in 'Tin Pan Alley'. 'Though I myself was never deeply religious,' he wrote in his autobiography, 'nor felt any sort of vocation for its work, the Salvation Army did leave me with a code of musical honesty and an overriding independence of thought in musical matters.'

In December 1916 he was called up into the 'other' Army but remained in England and gained still more musical experience in a military band. He was also introduced for the first time to smoking, visiting music halls, and taking out girls. After a brief spell in the Civil Service in 1919, Henry decided to enter show business playing the concertina. After a few engagements he formed a three-handed musical act called 'The Variety Three' which had a disastrous life and by the end of 1920 Harry Hall, as he billed himself, was a solo performer again, playing the piano in a cinema in Notting Hill Gate. To relieve the monotony he often played Chopin and Debussy as accompaniment to comedy 'silents' such as those featuring the Keystone Cops but nobody seemed to notice. During this period he managed to find time to take piano lessons at the Guildhall School of Music and just before Christmas 1922 Hall, heartily bored with cinema work, was persuaded by a friend to take a fortnight's temporary work as deputy pianist in the dance band of the Midland Hotel in Manchester. 'It was madness', Hall wrote later but he added 'Luckily I was mad.'

Quite naturally, Hall with his background of Salvation Army marches and silent film arrangements was rather lost in a dance band and proved something of an embarrassment to his friends who had got him the job. It looked as if his temporary engagement would be just that, when, in the best Hollywood Musical tradition, something happened. It was the night of the New Year's Eve Dance, and 'out front' were the cream of Manchester society and, more importantly, Arthur Towle, Managing Director of the Midland Hotels Group. An exhibition dance had been arranged by two leading professionals and the young lady in question – a Miss Harris – decided to change her costume between the waltz and the quick step. Sixty seconds had to be filled and the Musical Director whispered to Hall those time-honoured words of film dialogue, 'Play something quick!' Henry did and chose a showy Chopin study *The Butterfly*.

'I realized with a dazed feeling that something was happening. I was stopping the show for the first time in my life, the whole ballroom was applauding,' said Hall. 'Out front' Arthur Towle whispered to the Head Waiter 'We must keep that boy.' A few weeks later Henry Hall was leader of the band – the whole thing was like a script-writer's dream.

Less than a year later Hall was married, controlled five bands, and owned a Rover saloon – the page boy's ambitions were becoming reality. In his autobiography, Hall makes no secret of his cultivation of the rich and powerful. With the aid of the Head Waiter, the hotel hairdresser, and Dr Tommy Chaff, whom Hall described as 'a pillar of the Manchester social World', Henry got to know about, and be known by, everybody who mattered in the locality.

In 1924 Hall decided to transfer his own band from the Midland Hotel in Manchester to the new Gleneagles Hotel, replacing his band at the Midland with a new one. Gleneagles was to be an extra special hotel in the L.M.S. Group and Henry hit on the bright idea of broadcasting the opening night on the wireless. He managed to talk Herbert Carruthers, the B.B.C. Station Director at Glasgow, into arranging a relay and on 4 June 1924 Henry Hall and his band were heard on the air for the first time.

It was quite an achievement for it was the first time the B.B.C. had featured any dance orchestra except the Savoy Orpheans and the Savoy Havana Band. More broadcasts followed and so did a contract with Columbia Records. By 1932 Hall's band was being heard regularly on the air from the Gleneagles Hotel and the Midland Hotel in Manchester. Henry himself was controlling thirty-two bands by this time and relations with Arthur Towle and his son Geoffrey, who would succeed him as head of the L.M.S. Group, were becoming strained. Geoffrey Towle seemed to believe that it was the name of the L.M.S. Hotels which helped Hall rather than Hall's broadcasts helping the hotels.

It was in this atmosphere that Hall attended a meeting on 9 January 1932 at the B.B.C.'s Headquarters at Savoy Hill. He believed that its purpose was to discuss arrangements for more broadcasts from the Gleneagles Hotel. In fact they told him that Jack Payne was leaving the B.B.C. and asked Henry to replace him. They wanted an answer the same day and at first Hall was hesitant to give up the band organization he had so laboriously built up over the last ten years, but eventually he accepted – rather it seems to the B.B.C.'s surprise. The next day Hall parted company with Arthur Towle and the L.M.S. Group on the friendliest of terms, dined with Jack Payne at the Savoy Hotel, and signed a new contract with Columbia Records. He was thirty-three years old.

NA
LINE
C

*Henry on board the* Queen Mary, *May 1936.*

Now came the period of Hall's greatest success. He was a whole era – or rather the symbol of it – carnations in the button-hole, double-breasted tuxedos, and trips on the *Queen Mary*. He appeared so reassuring, tempering the inevitable glamour of a dance-band leader with those homely glasses that he always wore. And there was that signature-tune – 'Here's To The Next Time' – which presupposed that there would be a next time, that everything would carry on as before. The jaunty optimism of the composition is hardly surprising when one realizes that its original title was 'The Sunshine March' and that it had been composed by Hall in 1916 when he was working for the Salvation Army.

Hall was popular as his tumultuous reception at Radiolympia in 1932 proved. It was probably the last occasion that he would express surprise at his success – from now on he consolidated his position.

A trip to America in 1933 gave him several new ideas about records, music publishing, and radio presentation. He met the leaders of the entertainment industry and was dubbed by American newsmen 'The Rudy Vallee of England' – Henry thought it 'an amusing compliment'. At one famous New York night-club he was even announced as 'Sir Henry Hall, President of the British Broadcasting Corporation'. But perhaps the most interesting thing about the trip was the impression that the American radio announcers made on him – the way that 'in words apparently spontaneous yet which must have been carefully chosen, the announcer set the scene . . . and persuasively glamorized the whole proceedings'.

Until then announcements in his own programme had been made by his Manager. Now he decided that he would do them himself. 'I learnt to adapt a natural tendency to pause before words and stumble over them into a distinctive style which everybody knew,' he later wrote.

In 1934 came the next breakthrough with the first *Guest Night*, the show for which he is probably best remembered. Those hesitant and yet so deliberate words – 'This *is* Henry Hall speaking and tonight *is* my Guest Night' – launched a

*Henry at Waterloo Station on his return from America.*

whole new concept in broadcasting. It is easy to forget that he was the first person in Britain to use this formula that so many other people have come to rely on.

The first *Guest Night* on 17 March 1934 included Anona Winn, Elsie and Doris Waters, Flanagan and Allen, and Lupino Lane. They were followed a week later by Leslie Sarony, Layton and Johnstone, Doris Hare, and Ronald Frankau. It is difficult to name anybody in British show business from the 1930s to the 1950s who did not eventually appear in that programme.

Between 1934 and 1937 Hall enjoyed being a star. He made a film called *Music Hath Charms*, topped the bill at the London Palladium several times, and wrote some of his best numbers including 'It's Time to say Goodnight'. And there were more trips to America. But perhaps the most spectacular event of the period for Hall was the maiden voyage of the *Queen Mary* when he was engaged as Guest Conductor. He wrote a special signature-tune for the ship and called it 'Somewhere at Sea'. During the four-day voyage Hall and the special band led by Eddie Carroll broadcast fourteen times. When they arrived at New York they received a tumultuous reception and broadcast in a coast-to-coast radio link-up with a representative selection of the best bands of America. Again Hall met the leaders of the show-business and music-publishing world and returned to England full of enthusiasm for the way the American music industry worked.

On his immediate return to work and the preparation for the Christmas and New Year radio festivities, Hall had little time for reflection, but once 1937 had begun he realized that he and his orchestra had been with the B.B.C. for five years and that things were very different now to what they had been when he had joined the B.B.C. in 1932.

There were many bands competing on the air – those of Harry Roy, Sid Bright, Billy Cotton, Jack Payne, Ambrose, Geraldo, Felix Mendelsohn, Lew Stone, Nat Gonella, Brian Lawrence, Carroll Gibbons, and many more. In order to cope with this array of star bands, and as part of a new-look policy, Eric Maschwitz had broken the regular schedule of one band at one particular fixed time. Even the 5.15 to 6 p.m. spot was no longer exclusively Hall's, but open to everyone. Henry was uneasy and on 15 March, the morning of the fifth anniversary of his association with the B.B.C., he went to Sir John Reith's office and said, 'Sir John, with your permission I think I should like to go.'

Just as suddenly as he had made his decision to join the Corporation, Hall now decided to leave and, like Payne before him, to go into 'show business'. But Hall was able to get better terms than his predecessor.

Firstly, he and his band – the B.B.C. Dance Orchestra – would not be replaced and secondly, the entire music library of the B.B.C. Dance Orchestra was to be handed over free to Hall. It consisted of five thousand orchestrations which had cost approximately eight guineas each.

His final official programme took place on Saturday, 25 September 1937 and lasted from 10.40 till midnight. Its title was – of course – *Here's To The Next Time* and it consisted of a selection of the Orchestra's best numbers. Just for the record here is the list in full: 'The Teddy Bears' Picnic', 'Round the Marble Arch', 'Stormy Weather', 'It's a Sin to Tell a Lie', 'Come Ye Back to Bonnie Scotland' (Hall's old Gleneagles signature-tune), 'Butterflies in the Rain', 'I Cover the Waterfront', 'Red Sails in the Sunset', 'Misty Islands of the Highlands', 'Solitude', 'The Flying Trapeze', 'The Last Round Up', 'Goodbye Hawaii', 'Did You Ever

*Henry and his Orchestra in fine spirits, on the day they left the B.B.C.*

See a Dream Walking', 'On the Steamer Coming Over', 'Please', 'The Music Goes Round and Round', 'You're the Top', 'Little Man You've Had a Busy Day', 'Let's Put Out the Lights', 'Saddle Your Blues to a Wild Mustang', 'I Took My Harp to a Party', 'Lullaby of Broadway', 'In the Chapel in the Moonlight', 'The Fleet's in Port Again', 'Smoke Gets in Your Eyes', 'Is It True What They Say About Dixie', 'Rusty and Dusty', 'The Way You Look Tonight', 'Who's Afraid of the Big Bad Wolf', and 'The Leader of the Band' – Miss Gracie Fields came over from the London Palladium to close the programme with her rendering of 'You've Got to Smile When You Say Goodbye'.

The following Monday Henry Hall and his Orchestra opened at the Hippodrome in Birmingham and for the next two years they were a sensational success at every theatre they visited.

Now in December 1939 Henry Hall returned to the B.B.C. All theatres had been closed at the outbreak of war and when they did slowly begin

*Henry Hall and Lind Joyce in a wartime broadcast.*

to reopen in October and November 1939 they did so in conditions that were impossible for Hall's type of show. So he approached the B.B.C. 'I had been trying to have a word on the telephone with John Watt, B.B.C. Director of Variety, but they always said he was out', says Henry in his book, *Here's To The Next Time*. When he did eventually track him down in Bristol he was told that the programme schedule was too full to fit his orchestra in. What John Watt did mention, in passing, was that the B.B.C. hoped to use the Colston Hall in Bristol as a studio. What Henry didn't mention was that he had recently signed a contract giving him the sole use of that building. 'That was my cue to leave!' Henry wrote later, 'I went back to the farm and sat on my contract for the Colston Hall and waited for the phone to ring!'

Soon *Henry Hall's Guest Night* was broadcast every Thursday night at 8.30 p.m. 'from a stage somewhere in England' and continued to be heard throughout the war and long into the Television Age.

Henry Hall's career, from the moment he joined the Gleneagles Dance Band in 1924, was one success after another and Collie Knox, the famous Radio Critic, said in his book *People of Quality* that Hall was probably the only person 'who ever got exactly what he wanted from that extraordinary institution, the B.B.C'. He was probably right.

# 7. We'll Meet Again

Vera Welch was born in East Ham and was kept out of the school concerts because her voice was considered too low. Yet this girl would later be known to millions as Vera Lynn 'The Forces' Sweetheart'. She would also be the subject of frequent and bitter controversy for at least the first ten years of her career as a star.

Her background story is different from that of any of the other people in this book. There was no long career in 'the business'; none of the struggle and sacrifice before reaching the top. In newspaper interviews of the war period Vera had a stock summing-up which she delivered pat to journalists. It went like this: 'I sang a sad sort of song at a charity concert when I was seven and joined a juvenile troupe in which I was one of the Cracker Cabaret Kids. Later I sang for Howard Barker's Band; I was just sixteen!' We can fill in a few more details – Vera was fourteen when she left school. Howard Barker saw her doing a solo act at a dance at Poplar Baths when she was sixteen and offered her an engagement in his band and Vera's mother was on hand to make the arrangements there and then. By the time she was twenty she had moved to Ambrose's Orchestra by way of Billy Cotton, who had sacked her after three days because he thought her voice was unsuitable. It was when she was only twenty that she made a hit record called 'Red Sails in the Sunset' and was signed up by George Black for a show called *Applesauce* with Max Miller and Florence Desmond. Vera was amazed to find that she shared equal billing with them. By the age of twenty she had arrived.

It is to her credit that Vera did manage to reach the top before she was twenty-one *and* before the war broke out. It dispels the myth that Vera Lynn came to prominence only because of the special circumstances of war-time broadcasting. In fact the B.B.C. probably gained more from its association with Miss Lynn than she ever did. Her first solo broadcasts had begun in 1935 and by 1940 she was appearing in many programmes including *Ack-Ack Beer-Beer*, the special twice-weekly variety series for the men of Anti-Aircraft and Balloon Barrage Units. It was in this show that Vera met a B.B.C. producer called Howard Thomas, a recruit from commercial radio who had a great fascination for creating or 'putting over' personalities. In Vera Lynn, Thomas saw one thing above everything else – Vera was pleasant but not particularly glamorous, her voice was unusual and bands had to transpose her songs four or five keys down and she was only at home with very slow numbers but she did sound sincere and once you said that then all the 'disadvantages' of Miss Lynn became assets.

Together they worked out a formula for a show. Vera would write a letter to the Forces telling them about things back home, about their families and girl-friends. And the title? – it had to be *Sincerely Yours*.

> Dear Boys. . . . It used to be very easy to answer your letters because what most of you used to say was 'please send me your autograph or photograph'. But since I started my

Sunday broadcasts you've written to me very differently – as though you know me very well, as though I'm your friend . . .

The first programme of the *Sincerely Yours* series went out in November 1941. By 4 December of that year the Minutes of the Board of Governors of the B.B.C. contained this comment: '*Sincerely Yours* deplored, but popularity noted.'

So began the battle between the pro-Lynn faction, which consisted of the British Forces and most of the listening public, and the anti-Lynn camp, which consisted of nobody very much except a few arrogant old men who thought that the troops fought better on a diet of anti-German propaganda and military music.

Today, thirty years later, it may look as if Miss Lynn easily defeated her critics, but at the time there were strenuous efforts, both inside and outside the B.B.C., to at least get rid of *Sincerely Yours*, if not Miss Lynn herself.

By March 1942 Vera had become what is now called a 'superstar' and among a host of newspaper reports about her, Peter Stewart wrote in *Woman's Illustrated* of 'the girl whose lovely voice and quiet sincerity have made her the symbol of all the things we're fighting for'. That was what her opponents failed to grasp. They had excessive fears that Vera Lynn with her letter to 'The boys' and her news of wives, sweethearts, and babies would make the troops so homesick that they would lay down their arms and try to return home. But Vera credited the average British soldier with more sense than many people at the War Office did. She reminded them each week of just what they were fighting for and her broadcasts were listened to by the troops with far more respect and attention than the melodramatic exhortations of Mr Churchill – whose name they bracketed with that of Miss Gracie Fields as 'a good wireless turn'.

*Sincerely Yours* itself as a programme was, like all good ideas, very simple. It opened with Vera singing her signature-tune 'Wishing' and then, with the words 'Dear boys', she began her letter to the Forces, breaking it up with songs like 'I'll Be Seeing You' and 'Smiling Through'. And in the first series she would telephone hospitals, often right up to the time the programme was going on the air, to get news of new-born babies and pass it on to the fathers in the Forces. But it was more than just a good radio feature for Vera. As Wilfred Pickles has said, 'When Vera visited hospitals and then, on the Forces Programme, told the fighting men about their new babies, she was not merely

*Miss Lynn at a baby show.*

reading from a script; she really saw every child she talked about – and took flowers to all the mothers. Some people scoffed at this programme but to Vera it was a genuine job. And she did it well.'

Eventually, she had to drop this feature because she was being swamped by calls from hospitals, nursing-homes, midwives, and mothers and she just could not include all the messages in a half-hour programme. But then the whole programme was a message in itself and Vera spoke for everybody through her letter to the Forces. 'Of course we have to do it from a B.B.C. studio,' she told an *Empire News* reporter, 'but I try to imagine I am at my own fireside. When I sing to the boys I feel that I'm sort of in-between, I sing to *"her"* from *"him"*, and I tell one what the other wants to say. Perhaps they've had a quarrel or are shy; well the boy asks me to sing a special song because he knows his girl will hear it and know just what he means.'

Vera said that she was already receiving a thousand letters a week asking for advice on domestic problems and on Service questions, asking for help to find people the writers had lost touch with and, in one case, a letter from the crew of a minesweeper asking Vera to broadcast an S.O.S. for their ship's mascot – a ginger-brown terrier called Bobby.

Suddenly somebody had struck a chord in the heart of the Forces and they responded admirably. And Vera's sincerity paid huge dividends in terms of hard cash as well as fan-mail. During the year 1942 Eric Bennett, writing in the *Strand Magazine*, estimated her earnings from stage work, broadcasting, and gramophone records to be in excess of £700 a week and that she earned £6,000 per film (her first picture entitled *Sincerely Yours* was made in 1942), that would put her earnings for 1942 at over £42,000, which is

*Miss Lynn presents a mobile canteen to Forces, on behalf of the Variety Artists Ladies Guild.*

*The Forces Sweetheart.*

probably not far out considering that later in the war Vera was talking of earning £50,000 a year. To be fair, she also said that of that £50,000 she only retained £5,000 herself – 'it's very difficult to make £5,000 these days', she explained.

With the money she earned she bought a nine-roomed house in Barking and a little green seven-horsepower car but the rest went into War Bonds. As she told reporters, she had very few ambitions – her greatest one was to 'get fat'. It seemed that Vera, who in 1941 married Leading Aircraftman Harry Lewis whom she had met when he was playing the clarinet in Ambrose's Orchestra, was just a normal housewife who happened also to be a famous singer. Everybody was struck by the total absence of the usual trappings and attitude associated with stardom. Even when Vernon Bartlett, M.P. talked scathingly about 'sentimental, sloppy muck in the Forces Programme' and the B.B.C. announced that they would in future have programmes of a 'more virile nature', Vera was bewildered rather than annoyed.

Later when a former Minister, the Earl of Winterton, spoke of the 'caterwauling of an inebriated cockatoo' and its bad effect on military morale, Vera merely referred to her large volume of fan-mail, while Miss Anne Shelton replied 'It's a pity they can't get on with the war instead of worrying about soldiers' morale!' It was not clear in fact which of the two ladies Lord Winterton was referring to, and his views commanded scant respect anyway, but it was typical of the offensive remarks that both Vera Lynn and Anne Shelton were frequently subjected to.

It should be borne in mind that both these girls were in their early twenties when this barrage of abuse was being directed at them from M.P.s, ex-Ministers, and the retired military people who, in fact, one would have expected to have behaved more gallantly.

Miss Anne Shelton came off better than Vera though, because her numbers were more 'bright' and much of her repertoire consisted of 'simple marching songs'. But as Vera Lynn's radio producer, Howard Thomas, pointed out, Miss Lynn would not be so successful if she sang the 'bright' type of song that some of her critics wanted. After all, the outstanding song of the war, and one which was popular with fighting men of both Allied and Axis Forces, was 'Lili Marlene' – a composition much more in keeping with the style of Vera Lynn than of Anne Shelton.

But, although Vera had withstood general criticism for a long time and usually countered it with a disarming incomprehension of anybody who didn't like sentiment, by 1944 she was beginning to become very sensitive about being impersonated. In November of that year, the *Daily Express* reported that she had warned mimics that she would take action to stop them giving bad impersonations of her.

As early as 1942 Vera had been burlesqued by Dorothy Dickson in a London revue. By all accounts it was 'a wickedly funny act' to quote a contemporary report, 'the microphone magnified whine of her crooning and the studied monotony of gesture brought the house down: yet Vera Lynn wasn't even named'.

The description is Eric Bennett's who asked Vera about it in an article for the *Strand Magazine:*

> 'I haven't seen it,' the victim said, the smile disappearing and the mouth hardening. 'Some people say it's cruel, and if so that's wrong. I don't mean it's wrong making fun of *me* – but it is wrong to make fun of the things that

ordinary men and women like. Soldiers and their wives listen to the programmes at the same time. My songs bring them together . . . that's worthwhile isn't it?'

Bennett reflected that she appeared to have an almost Evangelical belief in the need for the sentiment that she sang. 'She just does not understand the people who dislike her songs', he concluded.

A few days after her 1944 warning in the *Daily Express*, the *Sunday Pictorial* reported that Vera was now threatening to take legal action against 'bad' mimics. In March 1945 an article written by Miss Lynn herself appeared in *Tit-Bits*. It was entitled 'A Joke I No Longer Enjoy' and Vera was now obviously furious about the whole issue. She elaborated on her now-familiar argument that any impersonation of her act was an attempt to belittle and ridicule the fighting men and the ordinary people of Britain. Her fans, she said, had written to her by the hundred telling her how much they disliked these impersonations and, as she owed everything to her fans, she explained, then it was her duty to discourage the practice.

The B.B.C. ruling was that mimics could only impersonate on the air those people who had given them permission to do so. Vera accordingly impressed on the Corporation that no such permission had been, or would be, obtained from her. 'But provided my name isn't mentioned', Vera complained, 'nothing can stop an artiste "playing herself on" to eight bars of "Yours" and proceeding to blather about "You dear boys", all of which imposes no great tax on the imagination of listeners.'

Now Vera hadn't the least objection, as she explained in her *Tit-Bits* article, to friendly, good-humoured impersonations. The problem was, however, that she didn't seem to see any like that. She quoted a hymn which she learnt at school about taking delight in simple things and 'mirth which hath no bitter springs' and reflected that few people took such excellent advice. 'Vera Lynn impressions can be sure to get a laugh,' she wrote, 'even, strangely enough, from my best friends.' Then Vera referred to a new aspect of the saga – money. Quite apart from the previous objections, these impersonations were damaging to her business as a singer. There were, she estimated, about one hundred theatres in Great Britain where she had not as yet appeared. 'If a Vera Lynn impersonator gets to these theatres before me, she provokes enough cheap ridicule to kill my act stone dead', said Miss Lynn.

She reflected that there were two ways of getting a laugh. One was 'taking a rise', as she put it, and the other was obscenity. It seemed that she considered the former more reprehensible and maintained that it was a form of slander for people to impersonate her – even though the law didn't recognize it as such. 'These impersonations represent an attack, not on my performance,' she argued, 'but on my sincerity', and there at least she had a valid point for it is quite obvious from reading Miss Lynn's opinions that she *was* sincere in her belief that her work was important.

I have been to Burma and I have studied reactions at first hand and what I've seen convinces me that my musical mission, however it may be viewed by artistic standards, is, in its own small way, important and I venture to prophesy that it will survive all the taunts and cruel impersonations to which it has been subjected.

*Vera Lynn in a war-time Forces broadcast.*

And in saying that Vera Lynn was certainly right. Unfortunately, however, the B.B.C. weren't quite so sure about Vera's musical mission as she was.

Once the war was over, the B.B.C., which had been used as an instrument of morale boosting and propaganda, no longer *had* to use Miss Vera Lynn. The war-time necessity of giving the soldiers and 'front-line civilians' what they wanted no longer existed and although she had a radio series in 1947, 1948, and 1949 when she replaced the phenomenal top-billing Donald Peers programme, Vera began to get upset about her treatment at the hands of the B.B.C.

She had good cause. Throughout the war she had been exploited as 'a symbol of what we are all fighting for'. Granted a good proportion of the Establishment had heartily professed to abhor all that Vera stood for, but they had at the same time found her very useful in helping to get the British Forces and public to win the war. Now she was being slowly frozen out – that certainly was her interpretation and on the evidence available it seems to be the correct one.

The year 1949 saw the triumph of Donald Peers and when his record-breaking radio series went off the air, Vera Lynn replaced it. She could hardly have been given a better peak listening time to fill but Donald Peers had been singing 'cheer-up' songs. 'In my songs I said that life's not so bad after all – and it paid off', he explained recently. Vera on the other hand was still singing the type of song that had been so popular with the troops overseas. The trouble was that although life was just as depressing and drab as it had been during the war – in fact materially things were much worse in 1949 than in 1942 – in the eyes of most people there was no reason why it should be so. The war had been over for four years but things showed no signs of getting any better. Vera might still be popular but her songs were not what the B.B.C. wanted. What was called for they felt was a different kind of morale boosting – people had to be 'buoyed-up'.

After the 1949 series there were to be no more regular broadcasts for Vera Lynn. The B.B.C. asked her to 'cheer-up her songs and scripts' but she refused.

In January 1951, therefore, a public row blew up between Vera and the Corporation. A *Daily Mirror* headline read 'Vera Beats B.B.C. Snub, To Sing For Forces'. What it meant was that Miss Lynn had at long last accepted commercial radio work and signed a contract for ten programmes to be entitled *Vera Lynn Sings*. The shows would be heard on Radio Luxemburg and afterwards the commercials would be removed and the programmes handed over to the War Office for use on Forces radio stations.

During the past year she had broadcast for the B.B.C. on only three occasions and Vera told the Press that she had received letters from all over the world asking why she was no longer broadcasting with the B.B.C. Even the War Office had approached her about it. 'I can't understand the B.B.C.'s attitude towards me. It's most humiliating,' she said.

Later in the year the B.B.C. did offer occasional broadcasts to Vera – on condition that she 'cheered-up' her material but she was not prepared to do so especially as she was now recording thirty-two programmes for Radio Luxemburg who were quite happy with her style as it was. The shows were heard on Forces radio stations from Hamburg to Hong Kong and the series was sold to Australia and Canada. In fact, 1951 was a very good year for Vera. She played to packed houses at the Opera House, Blackpool for seventeen weeks and went on to the London Palladium. She was in the Royal Command Performance and her records sold very well – at the end of 1951 her most recent recording 'If You Go' was a best-seller in both Britain and the United States. And in December 1951 Vera decided that she would cross the Atlantic. In an interview for *Reynolds News* she said:

> After Christmas I shall be leaving England for America. It will be a sad parting, for I leave many friends behind me. The truth is that I don't really want to go. I am too fond of England and English audiences. But I am going to sing on American Radio because of the stubbornness of the B.B.C., who have consistently snubbed me, ignored me, and given me the cold shoulder for three long years.

The newspapers carried the story of Vera's self-imposed exile during the Christmas period of 1951. *Reynolds News* headlined it with 'Why I Am Leaving, by Vera Lynn' while the *Daily*

*Mirror* played it for all it was worth with '"B.B.C. Is Turning Me Out" – Vera'. She had been offered a fee of £1,000 per radio performance by the National Broadcasting Company the *Daily Mirror* claimed.

It had all begun in the summer of 1951 when the N.B.C. decided to do their radio programme *The Big Show*, starring Tallulah Bankhead, from London. Vera Lynn was offered the vocal spot and sang one song. It so impressed N.B.C. officials that they offered 'the Forces' Sweetheart' four more appearances in America. And now she had accepted. But, as she said, she would much rather have stayed in England and sung on the B.B.C. – 'And I'm not after money. The paltry payments that the B.B.C. would hand over are not worth the work. Anyone will tell you that.' She wanted to work with the B.B.C. because the listeners wanted to hear her and Vera claimed that she received hundreds of letters every week asking why she wasn't broadcasting. And underneath all the anger and frustration was the same total incomprehension of the fact that anyone could *not* believe in her 'musical mission'. She asked:

> Why? I could understand if I were a flop, if my act were out of date. I could understand it if I had flopped in the dim and distant past when I *did* work for the B.B.C. But the B.B.C. made me. They built me up. I became the Forces' Sweetheart. They made millions of people my fans.

And she added the year 1951 had been her most successful ever. Every word of what she said was true. Now Vera had had enough of being told by B.B.C. producers that the public didn't want to hear her any more. 'It's made me very unhappy. I've upset myself too much,' she said. So Vera left for America where the N.B.C. signed her up on a four-year contract for *The Big Show* and the *Daily Mirror* hadn't been far out in its estimate about the broadcast payment. It was £735 per song.

On 18 July 1952 Vera Lynn, who was starring in *London Laughs* at the Adelphi, was given a gold record for selling 700,000 copies of 'Auf Wiedersehn Sweetheart' in one month. She not only topped the British Hit Parade but for the first time in history for a British artist, she topped the United States charts as well. The record had already earned $200,000 for Britain in four weeks and by the end of the year Vera Lynn was rated as one of Britain's top dollar-earning industries.

The record was, of course, slow, sad, and sentimental – just the sort of thing which the B.B.C. always *knew* the public didn't want any more. So naturally they didn't give her a radio series.

Few people in 1952 would have predicted that twenty years later, Vera Lynn would be starring in her own B.B.C. Television series.

*The BBC found it difficult to answer the radio attacks of William Joyce, known as Lord Haw-Haw. Eventually it was decided that the best policy was to reply with laughter. Here the famous Western Brothers are seen as The Führer (George) and Lord Haw-Haw (Kenneth).*

# 8. This is the B.B.C. *Light* Programme

When peace came in 1945 the B.B.C. had undergone a change even greater than that which the advent of widespread television-viewing was to bring about in the 1950s. Broadcasting House itself was no longer the white gleaming castle that Sir John Reith had moved into in 1932; rather it was now a grey battered fortress. It had suffered a direct hit from a 500-pound time-bomb on 15 October 1940. Having entered by a seventh-floor window and smashed its way through the walls of the fifth floor, the bomb had finally come to rest in the third-floor Music Library and exploded during the Nine O'Clock News. Listeners heard a vague thud, a slight pause, and then announcer Bruce Belfrage continued reading the News. However, seven members of the B.B.C. staff were killed.

On 8 December the same year the building was set on fire when a land-mine exploded in Portland Place. The fire raged for seven hours and Broadcasting House was deluged with water but even then there was no break in the service. But if Lord Reith's building could survive the war, his concepts of broadcasting could not.

Although the competition of commercial radio had been removed in 1939, it had been replaced by two alternatives – at first German broadcasts and, increasingly after 1942, American programmes. German propaganda was personified by William Joyce, an Irish-American who had become a German citizen before the war. Jonah Barrington, the Radio Critic of the *Daily Express*, dubbed him 'Lord Haw-Haw' and under this name he became known to millions of listeners who regularly tuned in to his broadcasts for a variety of reasons. Many said it was because he was so funny although some said that they listened to hear the truth – one thing was certain, he was difficult to answer. Norman Birkett, the famous lawyer, did try but, as he explained to the B.B.C., 'Many of the criticisms of Haw-Haw, for example, are directed to our domestic affairs. The unemployment figures, the conditions revealed by the Evacuation Scheme, the evasion of Income Tax, and similar matters are typical. Now these subjects are those which many social workers have examined for many years.'

Ultimately, the B.B.C. decided that the only way to combat Lord Haw-Haw, to whom a third of the population admitted being regular listeners, was to win the audience back with really popular shows. The programme schedules were rearranged to capture the listeners before Lord Haw-Haw broadcast, with variety shows such as *Bandwagon* and stars like Gracie Fields and Vera Lynn being used to hold them while the German programme was on the air.

Just when better programme-planning combined with good war news had managed to win back the B.B.C.'s listeners, a new transatlantic rival began to appear. Curiously enough it was the B.B.C., in the shape of John Watt's Assistant Director, Pat Hillyard, who first introduced American radio shows to Britain. Hillyard went to the U.S.A. in 1942 with the specific task of bringing back writers and stars 'to infuse new life and competition into our present set-up'. By 1943 many well-known American shows and performers were being broadcast by the B.B.C. including Irving Berlin's show *This Is The Army* and artists such as Jack Benny, Bob Hope, and ventriloquist Edgar Bergen.

*Vic Oliver (right) welcomes Bob Hope to a* Variety Bandbox *show.*

By 1944 the B.B.C. was plainly worried and the Director-General expressed fears of the American material becoming a Frankenstein monster and ordered that there should be no more American shows introduced without reference to him.

By then, of course, it was too late – not only was the B.B.C. Forces Programme carrying a large amount of American material but the American Forces Network was also now providing an alternative service which could be heard in many parts of Britain. The final blow to Reithian radio was delivered by General Eisenhower who used his influence with Churchill to override the B.B.C.'s objections to a combined Anglo-American-Canadian Forces programme. The radio series, whether it be comedy, music, or soap-opera, was here to stay and when the General Forces Programme closed down on 28 July 1945 it was replaced the next day by the 'Light Programme'. Twelve years previously, the B.B.C. hadn't even had a separate Variety Department.

The war had brought to prominence some new stars whose shows were to be carried on in peacetime. *Merry Go Round* was undoubtedly the best example of this. The programme in fact consisted of three shows which the different branches of the Services contributed in turn. Eric Barker was the star of the Navy edition; Charlie Chester represented the Army, and the Royal Air Force had a well-established star in Richard Murdoch who was now teamed with Kenneth Horne. Their mythical R.A.F. station in 'Laughter Command' was called 'Much Binding in the Marsh' and when peace came the personnel at Much Binding merely transferred to civilian activities. Murdoch and Horne, who met when they served together in the R.A.F., had very different backgrounds. Dickie Murdoch had started in the chorus and became a leading figure in musical comedy and revue before *Bandwagon* made a radio star of him. Kenneth Horne, however, was the son of a Congregationalist minister and M.P., and he combined a radio career with being a Director of Triplex Safety Glass and various associated companies. Like Murdoch, he was at Cambridge University where he was a tennis blue, and during

*The* Much Binding in the Marsh *team, left to right, Kenneth Horne, Richard Murdoch, Maureen Riscoe, Sam Costa, and Maurice Denham.*

*Charlie Chester 1947*

the war as Wing-Commander Horne he worked with Squadron-Leader Murdoch to write *Much Binding in the Marsh*.

In the show with them was Sam Costa, whom they had also met in the R.A.F., and Maurice Denham who, like Costa, was a recruit from *ITMA*. Their post-war adventures included running the Much Binding Country Club (in a Nissen hut) and publishing the newspaper *The Weekly Bind* with Miss Gladys Plumb (Dora Bryan) as its Fashion Editress and Prudence Gush (none other than Sam Costa) as its Radio Critic.

For a time the team appeared in a *Much Binding* series on Radio Luxemburg which annoyed the B.B.C. no end. But so great was the programme's appeal, that the Corporation readily came to terms with the rebels and allowed them back on its air waves.

Charlie Chester's *Stand Easy* was mainly a vehicle for 'Cheerful Charlie' himself, who had made his first stage appearance at the age of seven in a children's concert at the Winter Gardens, Eastbourne and gone on to win eighty-two talent contests before breaking into 'the business' by way of the concert party and eventually the music hall. To many people Chester in his early days resembled a combination of George Formby, Tommy Trinder, and Max Miller and his bill-matter of 'Cheerful Charlie Chester' did tend to confirm the Millerish image. But the happy-go-lucky lunacies of *Stand Easy* established Chester as a star in his own right.

It was as Sergeant Chester of the Royal Irish Fusiliers that he was asked to write the Army contribution to the *Merry Go Round* series, and in that first programme he included Arthur Haynes who remained in the show for its entire life. Other members of the team were singer Fred Farrari, Len Marten, a straight actor from

*Pearl Hackney and Eric Barker 1946.*

'rep', Ken Morris, the musician and composer of the team who also wrote songs with Chester himself, and Edwina Carol who joined the show in 1948 and played Chester's secretary.

Eric Barker, the star of the Naval contribution to *Merry Go Round* was born in Surrey and his first job was in his father's wholesale paper business. He had already had three novels and several short stories published before he turned to the stage, first appearing as a character actor with the Birmingham Rep, and later as an impressionist at the Windmill Theatre.

During the war he served in the Royal Navy for five and a half years and became a major radio star. His *Merry Go Round* programme was followed by several others, much in the same

*Ben Lyon and Bebe Daniels.*

vein, including *Waterlogged Spa* and *Just Fancy*, in which he appeared with his wife Pearl Hackney.

Many other war-time shows survived into peace-time, notably *Music While You Work* and *Workers' Playtime*, both of which were leading examples of a large number of shows conceived solely to increase production. *Music While You Work* was launched on 23 June 1940 with the enthusiastic backing of Lord Beaverbrook, Minister of Aircraft Production, and Ernest Bevin, Minister of Labour, and *Workers' Playtime* was first heard on 31 May 1941. Again Bevin was very much in favour of it and the show had grown from an idea of John Watt to broadcast an edition of *Garrison Theatre* from a factory. Other shows of the same type were *Factory Canteen* and *Works Wonders* where the acts were provided by the workers themselves.

The only other major war-time show to gain a large following was *Happidrome* which chronicled the adventures of two idiots, Enoch (Vincent Robinson) and Ramsbottom (Cecil Frederick), and the quick-witted Mr Lovejoy (Harry Korris). Their song 'We Three in Happidrome' was sung by nearly everyone and is even occasionally heard today. *Happidrome*, however, was in the British music-hall tradition and owed nothing to American influences – it did not survive the war.

The new Light Programme, while retaining a great deal of war-time material, managed in a very short period to create a large number of new series which were to lay the foundation of its programme-content until the 1960s. In doing this it also created new stars and, at the same time, completely altered the nature of 'show business' as a whole.

Before the war, the theatre and music-hall world had often dictated to the B.B.C. Broadcasting had, at the most, been a small branch of 'the business'. Now it was to become the central feature of entertainment. Radio created the stars and the impresarios were content to follow the B.B.C.'s lead and book radio artists in the sure knowledge that they meant 'house full' notices.

The Light Programme was born in 1945; ten years later the first commercial television station would go on the air. That event would spell not only the end of the B.B.C.'s monopoly of broadcasting but the fact that radio would suddenly change overnight from being the big brother of broadcasting to being the poor relation.

But it was a glorious ten years and during the decade a whole firmament of show-business stars was created. Of course, Henry Hall, the Lyons, Tommy Handley, and all the war-time heroes carried on, but new names like Ted Ray, Donald Peers, Tony Hancock, Frankie Howerd, Max Bygraves, Archie Andrews and Peter Brough, and the Goons appeared too. And so did the serial. The war had produced *The Robinson Family* but now came *P.C. 49*, *The Daring Dexters*, *Adventure Unlimited*, *Journey Into Space*, *Mrs Dale's Diary*, *Riders of the Range*, *The Archers*, and most significant of all, *Dick Barton*, the serial which was really responsible for all the rest.

The stage was set then, in 1945, for whoever wanted to use it. It only needed someone with enough gumption to 'have a go'.

ARE YE COURTING!
BBC

# 9. Have A Go

One of the interesting things about post-war Britain was the way in which it chose idols who reflected the over-all mood of the nation. And the mood was one of austerity, shortages, and sacrifice. The American radio stars were people like Bob Hope, Burns and Allen, Joan Davis, Jack Benny, and singers like Rudy Vallee, Bing Crosby and, of course, the young Sinatra. Their shows (with the exception of Sinatra's) dated from at least the mid 1930s and the artists were as much products of Hollywood as they were of radio. It was not surprising, therefore, that there was a certain aura of glamour surrounding the American broadcasters, who were able to obtain clothes, petrol for their cars, and as much meat as money could buy without having to worry about ration books.

Here in Britain things were different. The entertainment world shared the shortages that everybody suffered – and to do otherwise would have been disastrous. Ivor Novello had gone to prison during the war when a woman fan had fraudulently obtained an extra petrol ration for him. Even the dummy Archie Andrews had to have a ration book for clothing. Perhaps the dance-band leaders still managed to appear glamorous – they always did – but most artists, like Vera Lynn, looked and dressed very much as their public.

In these conditions circumstances dictated that the 'star' must also seem to be 'the common man', and waiting in the wings was someone who had been rehearsing that particular role for several years. Indeed, in the late 1940s the mere mention of 'the common man' would have been sufficient to introduce the broadcaster who became the biggest audience attraction in the history of British radio.

With his famous 'Ow do, 'ow are yer?' Wilfred Pickles introduced the legendary *Have A Go* each week to an audience of twenty million, almost all of whom adored him. In almost every aspect of show business he was a superstar who at one time was appearing in three radio and one television series each week and topping the bill both in the music hall and as a straight actor in the 'legitimate' theatre. He even played dramatic roles in the Third Programme and gave a radio series of poetry readings that were wildly successful. His books, and there were several, were inevitably best-sellers. The first, an autobiography entitled *Between You and Me*, was reprinted eight times within three months of publication. And amazingly there seemed to be no sign of an end to it. Pickles just got bigger and bigger. The B.B.C., of course, helped the process along and then got caught up in the uncontrollable momentum of this juggernaut. There is a photograph on the first page of a 1950 *Radio Times* which rather sums up the Corporation's attitude to Wilfred. It was taken at the Royal Mint and showed a large pair of scales – Wilfred is sitting on one side and a huge pile of sovereigns is on the other. The caption, of course, reads 'Worth His Weight in Gold' – at least it was frank.

*Wilf and Mabel congratulate a jackpot winner. On the left seated is ninety-three year-old Mr James Rickard.*

The Pickles' recipe had, as its basic ingredient, a collection of widely held public articles of faith, such as the theory of the superiority of 'ordinary' people over all other kinds; the idea that the remoteness of a locality was in direct proportion to the interest of its inhabitants, that to endure hardship was both laudable and good for the character, and that old age was a truly remarkable and praiseworthy achievement.

Added to this were Pickles's own ideas – though hardly exclusive to him – that everybody had a story to tell and that even the dullest occupation yielded the occasional interesting experience. However, these ideas were the basis of all 'meet the people' shows.

To this, Pickles and his team added the competitive instinct and the chance of winning a small sum of money and mixed the whole thing with a massive dose of sentiment. The result was 'instant radio' and an overnight success of frightening proportions.

Having said all that, may I now add that the programme *Have A Go* was one of the finest examples of how to use radio; that the show did have a tremendously beneficial effect on its millions of listeners, and that Pickles was the only man who could have compèred the programme and made it work.

Pickles was born in Halifax in 1904 and very early in life gained the outlook that was to make him 'a natural' for broadcasting. He had an aunt, of whom he was very fond, who hadn't learnt to read but she encouraged young Wilfred to read to her – another aunt had the ability to make very ordinary events sound gripping, graphic adventures – both were to help make Wilfred an excellent story-teller. The rest of the large working-class family of uncles and aunts provided him with ample opportunity for character study. It greatly upset him, however, that his father, who had a reputation as a gifted wit and mimic, spent so little time at home and preferred to be 'out with the boys'. Wilfred determined that he would not make the same mistake.

Early in the First World War, Pickles senior joined up and things were particularly hard for the family at home. Wilfred, then aged twelve, longed to get a job so that he could help the family finances – the mills especially attracted him. To him they were things of unique beauty – anything but 'dark and satanic'. In winter their light lit up Halifax making the wet pavements glister and the streets appear friendly. 'I used to stand and feel an admiration for the people who kept the mills going and I longed to be in there with them.'

But although twelve-year-old Wilfred was offered a job as a 'half-timer' at the Blackburn and Bray Mill, his mother refused to let him start work there and instead he became a part-time errand-boy at Mitchells, a ladies' and gents' outfitters in Halifax. Eventually, he became a shop-assistant and was very well thought of by his employer, but when the war ended, his father returned from the Army and decided to start his own business as a builder with Wilfred as his first labourer. The new job didn't much appeal to young Pickles who was now thoroughly stage-struck and had taken to trying to fool Halifax theatre queues by walking briskly past them with his collar turned up in the hope that they would think he was an actor.

From his wages, he saved five shillings to buy *The Works of Shakespeare* and one night read part of them to his mother. Suddenly she got up and said 'I think you'd better 'ave some lessons in acting, lad.' So young Wilfred was sent to a Congregationalist minister who enjoyed some local fame for his marathon recitations of Dickens. Here he learnt elocution and began to take part in Sunday School concerts and the like, but already he was beginning to reject the then fashionable style of recitation which was always accompanied by extravagant arm movements. Wilfred thought that all the interpretation should come from the inflexions of the voice.

At eighteen Wilfred joined a group of friends to form an amateur dramatic society and made the acquaintance of a school-friend of his brother Arthur, a young man named Eric Portman. When, a few months later, Portman joined a professional theatrical company that had been visiting Halifax, Wilfred was filled with admiration and envy. About this time the Pickles family moved to Southport where the leading lights of the amateur dramatic society were a family called Myerscough. He found out their address and paced up and down outside their house one Sunday morning. But on this occasion, Wilfred's interest in acting took second place, for he was hoping to catch a glimpse of the Myerscoughs' daughter, Mabel. Her younger brother, John, spotted Wilfred, whom he had seen at rehearsals and asked him in and, within four months, Wilfred and Mabel were engaged.

Mabel was a great devotee of the Liverpool Repertory Company and she and Wilfred attended their productions every Saturday evening. After one particular show Wilfred told Mabel that he would like to try and get a job with the Company but she advised against it and thought he'd do better on radio. 'There's a real opportunity there,' she said.

Wilfred and Mabel were married on 20 September 1930 and it was another two years before Wilfred actually did try to get some radio work. Then after hearing a play on the wireless and being told by Mabel that he could do much better himself, Wilfred wrote for an audition with the B.B.C.'s North Region. He got his audition which was a success and from then on radio work came thick and fast. It was pretty varied stuff, plays, Children's Hour, poetry, and even variety shows but Wilfred enjoyed it all and met in those early days many of the people who would later help him shape *Have A Go*.

By 1938, Wilfred was beginning to feel rather restless about his role with the B.B.C.; there was plenty of broadcasting work available but he felt that there was no security attached to it. He toyed with the idea of leaving but once again Mabel was ready with the correct advice; 'We'll regret it if you don't stick at it. I still think you've got something for radio they haven't discovered yet!' And ironically Wilfred's thoughts at this time were dwelling on the people that he passed each day on his way to Broadcasting House in Manchester. 'My curiosity about these folk increased,' he wrote in his autobiography, 'I wanted to follow them home, eat with them, and have a chat with them about what they wanted to do with their lives. . . . I vowed I would try to find the answers to all my questions.' But it didn't occur either to him or to Mabel that this curiosity was the 'something for radio' that Wilfred had got to offer.

A few months later he was given a job as an announcer in the North Region and on Mabel's advice he used his Northern accent although by now he was quite capable of adopting any dialect that he chose. Soon afterwards war broke out and it was at this time that their young son David contracted infantile paralysis and died. It affected them deeply and anyone reading Pickles's account of the loss of his only child can see why he was later to take such a genuine interest in entertaining children in hospital.

As the B.B.C. got into its stride with war-time broadcasting, Wilfred's position within the Corporation's North Region improved. He was now on the permanent staff at a salary of £480 a year and apart from announcing he became involved in a number of programmes such as *Kingpins of Comedy*, a fifteen-minute show in which he interviewed famous comedians of the day. At about this time Wilfred received a visit from an invalided soldier who had been injured at Dunkirk. They met when he had done some freelance broadcasting for the North Region's Children's Hour before the war. Now he told Wilfred that he would return to his pre-war job of selling boilers but Pickles dissuaded him and offered to coach him as an announcer. After a few trial runs the twenty-one-year-old soldier made a test recording and Pickles was told to engage him on the spot – his name was Robert Robinson.

*Kingpins of Comedy* had proved to be such a success that North Region producer, Geoffrey Brisdon, decided to give Wilfred another programme of his own. Brisdon's idea was to revive a feature called *Harry Hopeful* that he had created some years before. In it, Frank Nichols, who had been a friend of Wilfred's in the early 1930s, had played the part of 'a happy-go-lucky character who had wandered round the country meeting ordinary people and bringing them to the microphone in their natural environment'. Of course a new name was needed. Brisdon and Wilfred's fellow announcers, Ralph Truman and Robert Robinson racked their brains but failed to come up with an answer and then one evening as he was returning home by bus Wilfred passed a chapel in Oxford Road, Manchester. Over the door was an enormous sign saying 'YOU ARE WELCOME'. By the time he had got home Wilfred had thought up a Christian name to match and as 'Billy Welcome' he began his travels all over Britain. Much of the type of material that would later make *Have A Go* such a success was heard in the early *Billy Welcome* programmes and Wilfred was obviously doing what he wanted to do, even though his role as compère seemed out of step with the Pickles' philosophy of life. Billy Welcome was an idle work-shy wanderer who asked people about their jobs and made a great play of finding excuses for why he couldn't do them himself. And although, as I have said, the basic *Have A Go* material was already there in *Billy Welcome* the presentation was lacking. Recordings of the show often reveal painfully long pauses while interviewees turned over pages of a script and there was a total lack of spontaneity. Even Wilfred sounded ill at ease in some editions of the programme. As the series progressed and as the B.B.C. saw the morale-boosting potential of a 'meet the people' show its basic concept changed. *Billy Welcome* was moved to munition factories and the like, and a studied heartiness and 'we can take it' spirit was injected. 'It was rank propaganda,' Pickles wrote, and said that it disturbed him to have to go into industrial canteens and work up a frenzy of patriotism, national fervour, and a go-to-it spirit among the workers. Pickles wrote:

> I hated the job. There were marching songs and sentimental melodies. I had to ask such questions as 'Are we afraid of Hitler?' and 'Can we lick him?' And there were personal endeavour stories.... 'Looking after three children and still doing a grand job in the factory. Good Lass', I would say, giving her a pat on the back. How I loathed it and how embarrassed I felt.

He would have been happier if he had been allowed to explain to 'those grand folk' that he was there to help them work harder and increase their confidence.

Apart from *Billy Welcome*, Wilfred was still engaged on *Kingpins of Comedy* and various other programmes when John Snagge telephoned him from London one day to tell him that he wanted him to join the News-reading team there.

From that moment on Pickles changed from being a well-known all-rounder in the B.B.C. North Region to a national celebrity. His appointment as a News-reader and the fact that he intended to use his Northern accent caused a Press sensation. The idea had come, not from John Snagge, but from Brendan Bracken, the Minister of Information, who felt that listeners might be getting tired of Oxford accents. But there was another important consideration –

Bracken thought that Wilfred's accent would be more difficult for the Germans to imitate. With the new job came an increase in salary to £800 a year as well as a national reputation and Pickles managed to end his first News Bulletin with 'good neet'.

But although he was a great success in his new role he longed to get back to Manchester and after a few months it was quietly arranged that he should return to the North Region and continue *Billy Welcome, Kingpins of Comedy,* and *Two's a Crowd,* a comedy show in which he starred with Jack Train. As if this wasn't enough, Wilfred managed to persuade John Sharman to give him a spot on the B.B.C.'s *Music Hall* programme and, with commendable frankness, Pickles tells us in his book *Between You and Me*:

> The after-effects of my initiation as a radio comedian did not end with fan-mail and praise from my B.B.C. colleagues: practically every agent in London wrote suggesting that if I could continue to turn out material like I had used in my spot on *Music Hall* there was a chance for me on the variety stage.

Sunday concerts followed and in February 1943 Wilfred and Mabel went to see Julius Darewski the agent and asked him what he could do for them. He immediately offered a season at the Blackpool Opera House, followed by a music-hall tour and, at Christmas, a Tom Arnold pantomime. After a brief discussion, Pickles signed a contract and gave a month's notice to the B.B.C. It seems unnecessary to add that the Blackpool show was a great success. Wilfred topped a bill that included Rawicz and Landauer, Jewell and Warris, Elisabeth Welch, and the Dagenham Girl Pipers.

The pantomime at Liverpool, *Sleeping Beauty,* was followed by the offer of the lead in *The Cure For Love* which was running at the Westminster Theatre and Pickles eagerly took over the role created by Robert Donat. At the same time Geoffrey Brisdon of the B.B.C. North Region created another radio series for Pickles called *Ex-Corporal Wilf* in which he set out to show the problems confronting demobilized soldiers.

The war over, Pickles hovered between stage and radio work. Walter Greenwood had asked him to play in the provincial tour of *The Cure for Love* and he was on the point of accepting when John Salt of the B.B.C. telephoned him and said that he had an idea for an important programme.

*Wilfred, right, with a contestant.*

*Wilfred, Radio's North Star, as he was billed, visits a factory.*

'It's amazingly simple really,' Salt told Wilfred as he outlined his plans for a quiz show which would be unscripted and, unlike its American models, broadcast from a different place every week. 'And interview ordinary folk,' Wilfred enthused. 'Most certainly,' Salt replied and that was that. 'Amazingly simple' John Salt had said and amazingly simple it was, but then most good ideas are. A private recording was arranged so that the team could iron out any problems before going ahead with the real thing. There were some differences of opinion, however, between Pickles and John Salt who insisted on using a small orchestra led by Jack Jordan. Jordan and Philip Robinson, who was to be the show's original Producer, had meanwhile thought up a title for the programme. It was 'Quiz Bang'. 'I'm sorry,' said Pickles, 'but I won't appear in any programme called "Quiz Bang".' Rather taken aback, they asked him for a better suggestion. 'Where it came from I don't know,' Pickles wrote later, but he found himself saying 'Have A Go, Joe.' When, after the show's tremendous success in the North Region, it was decided to broadcast it nationally on the Light Programme, 'Joe' was dropped from the title.

Anyone looking back on those early days of *Have A Go* may now find it difficult to believe that the show had a regular audience of twenty million people – more than ITMA or any other wireless programme had managed to achieve – but this was no less than the truth.

Today the quiz show is an essential ingredient of television programming and Hughie Green, who has the greatest claim of anyone to be Pickles's spiritual successor, can point to the fact that his show has never left the Top Ten ratings in the seventeen years of its existence. But in the B.B.C. of the 1940s quiz shows were still slightly novel. Reith had forbidden them, except in *Children's Hour*, and they had only been allowed to creep into the programme schedule during the war.

It would be wrong, however, to see *Have A Go* as *just* a quiz show. The three or four questions that Pickles asked the contestants (perhaps participants is a better word) were incidental to the general purpose of the programme which was to talk to 'ordinary folk' about their everyday lives. The quiz was simply a device used to get people

*Wilfred prepares for a factory edition of* Have A Go *in early 1947.*

before the microphone, and early in the programme's history Pickles decided to 'give 'em the money' even if they didn't answer the questions correctly. It is doubtful whether, even in the bleak late 1940s, the prospect of someone winning a guinea at the rate of five bob an answer really had people on the edge of their seats. And the jackpots, which usually consisted of sums like 34*s*. or absurd combinations of 19*s*. 11½*d*. and an old gas-mask, look rather silly today when a programme like *Sale of the Century* regularly gives away £1,000 a week.

The magic of *Have A Go* – and the success of the show must have seemed truly magical to the B.B.C. – lay in its ability to 'Bring the people *to* the people' to quote one of the programme's slogans. Perhaps for the first time, members of the public broadcast in their own right, speaking not from a script but, as Pickles might have said, from their hearts. It had never been done before, at least not in Britain and, had it not been for Pickles, it might never have been done at all. That was his contribution to the story of broadcasting in Britain. And although *Have A Go*, like all shows, had a vast number of back-room boys who enjoyed none of the praise and glamour that the programme gave Wilfred, he was after all the only person with the ability to pull it off.

If the programme wallowed in sentimentality, and it did, then all the more credit to Pickles for being able to make it credible and acceptable to both the audience and the B.B.C. hierarchy. And if in some instances it teetered dangerously on the brink of bad taste, Pickles always managed to pull it back to the safe ground of 'the earthy natural simple humour of the British people' as one fan-letter described it.

Its listeners were drawn from every possible social group. Pickles spoke of 'lords and labourers, knights and knocker-uppers' making up his audience but there were several million people in between. One letter he received from an exile in Khartoum began:

> I have knocked about the world quite a lot, so I'm not exactly a namby-pamby but, dash me, you can make me weep and laugh. The B.B.C. have got it into their skulls that we abroad like high-class stuff and do they dish it up! – but I, like the majority, never miss, if possible, *Have A Go*.

One could quote endlessly from letters written by children, old-age pensioners, invalids, parents, soldiers, miners, even from expatriate Britons behind the Iron Curtain but they would all say, in their different ways, one thing – that *Have A Go* was the highlight of their week. For some, particularly the old or the sick, it even became the highlight of their lives. Such was the popularity of the show – and the power that Pickles could wield whenever he chose to.

When the programme visited St George's Crypt, Leeds, a haven for down-and-outs and tramps, Pickles showed them as they were, hopeless, bewildered, and pathetic. There was no suggestion of sending money to the organizers of the place – nothing was further from his mind – but Wilfred ended the broadcast by saying 'Remember these people in your prayers.' Almost immediately an avalanche of clothes poured in and so did donations of money adding up to £3,000. The B.B.C. were alarmed and annoyed. They were even more annoyed when he interviewed a young ex-R.A.F. pilot who had been badly injured and had been operated on more than thirty times. He had gone in for bulb-growing but in the programme he told Wilfred that business was not so good. That was enough for Wilfred who said to his twenty

million audience 'If you want any bulbs write to Paul Hart of Spalding. He had a go. Why don't you have a go?' Any more, the B.B.C. said, and Pickles would get the sack. Later the Corporation decided that the show would no longer be allowed to visit hospitals. Now it was Wilfred's turn to be annoyed. If only, he thought, the men who made the restrictive decisions at the B.B.C. could get out and meet the people as he had done. But then his mind was dwelling a lot on the lines of 'if only'. If only the young people of London could be taught how to enjoy themselves healthily instead of wasting their lives in 'the diseased carcass of the West End', an area that he described as 'crudely nauseating' and a 'demoralizing district'. With Mabel he visited Sweden and found that nauseating too – Stockholm was 'the capital of mediocre modernity' and Sweden 'a country with its self-respect gone to seed'. There was plenty of food in the shops – 'steaks for the asking and cream cakes by the windowful' – but he found no signs of happiness there; the people were sullen and unco-operative. When he went to a dance-hall he was astonished to find more men there than girls. 'Suddenly I realized what the attrition of war had meant to our country, and what non-participation had done to the Swedes' self-respect.' If only they had been in the war.

He visited America too and broadcast on commercial radio. Needless to say he didn't like the set-up there and wrote three articles for the *Radio Times* giving his views on the subject. But although he wasn't impressed by American radio, it was very impressed by him: he claimed that its executives had said that *Have A Go* was the only thing that could bring American radio back to sanity.

Back in Britain he experienced his first real opposition from an audience when he took *Have A Go* to Glasgow University during Rag Week. He already wondered whether students should be allowed to 'inflict their extremes of humour on the rest of the community'. He was prepared for trouble but it gradually dawned on him that 'those students were out to wreck the show'. They booed, jeered, whistled, catcalled, and threw all manner of objects on the stage. Violet Carson, at the piano, was given a particularly rough time. Wilfred was all the more determined that the show should be broadcast and it went over the air with a constant barrage of boos and jeers. It was exactly what Pickles wanted his millions to hear. For weeks afterwards letters protesting at the behaviour of the students poured in from all over Britain.

*Leaving for America.*

*Receiving mail.*

Wilfred was never happier than when he was among his own people – 'ordinary folk'. He idolized them and they returned the compliment. For someone who began life stage-stuck his views had changed considerably. He could no longer stand actors off stage. He found them 'artificial, prosaic, and egotistical'; they set his nerves on edge. Television affected him the same way. 'Tinsel glamour', 'toothpaste smiles', 'dressing up', 'stagey artificiality' were his impressions of the new medium. It didn't compare with the old man who told Wilfred in *Have A Go* that his favourite drink was 'tea – with cenipods' – thus gaining incidentally the longest audience laugh ever heard in the history of British radio.

Pickles felt that nobody in the media understood the true spirit of 'the people'. He persuaded the *Daily Herald* to let him write a series of articles on the real state of the nation's morale and he undertook a variety of other radio and television shows that all involved meeting the people and hearing their views. Mabel warned him, 'They'll make a politician of you yet.' Lady Astor voiced the same sentiment when she said, 'Don't ever let them make a politician of

*Wilfred at a NATO exhibition in 1953.*

you. They'll try, you know.' He was a friend of Harold Wilson, then President of the Board of Trade, and an admirer of Winston Churchill but, although he admitted to having strong political convictions, he could not support a political party. Perhaps his political ideas went beyond mere party considerations.

'Wouldn't it be wonderful', he said to Mabel, 'if we could do a programme to show the world just what we're like in Britain. And then a portrait of Canada. Then the Australians and Norwegians. And the Dutch.' He was reminded of a letter from a Swede who told him that *Have A Go* was doing more than any ambassador could do in binding the nations together.

'In the hearts and voices of ordinary men and women was a key to peace', he said on the last page of his autobiography. In their voices was 'the one answer to the conquest of distance and the carrying capacity of bombers'. He mused about the people of Merseyside, Melbourne, and Moscow. He believed a world-wide *Have A Go* was the answer. Perhaps he was right. One thing is certain though, such a programme would never have been permitted.

There was a brief period when Pickles was more powerful than anybody else in Britain, when had he chosen, or perhaps had someone chosen for him, he could have moved into politics as Ronald Reagan did later in America. His appeal was enormous and his sentiments and opinions found an echo in the hearts of the vast majority. But he didn't make the move – perhaps he never wanted to. Instead he occupies a unique place in the history of British broadcasting.

Despite his deep hatred of 'pretentious' people (the most common adjective in his books), Pickles was, as far as I can tell, a genuine warm-hearted and generous man. I heard a recording of an early *Have A Go* and found myself marvelling at the way his complete sincerity still came over after twenty-four years. 'Ladies and Gentlemen of Ebbw Vale, 'Ow do and 'ow are yer?' The greeting was drowned in tumultuous applause as he introduced 'another half hour of homely fun, entirely spontaneous and unrehearsed'. The highlight of the show was provided by the old lady of eighty-six who was asked who she would like to be if she could be somebody else. 'Princess Elizabeth,' she replied. When Wilfred had finally managed to quieten the delighted audience, he asked her why. 'Nylon stockings,' she replied simply. The audience went wild with pleasure.

At that moment I could see Wilfred's point.

DICK BARTON
RULES OF CONDUCT
BBC

# 10. Dick Barton – Special Agent

As the clock ticked on towards 6.45 on any week-day evening in 1947 a stranger to Britain would have noticed a very curious phenomenon. Children who a few minutes earlier had been playing in the streets would disappear indoors; in boarding-schools all over the country 'prep' would be halted and youngsters everywhere would suddenly draw closer to the wireless and try to cloak their excitement with a façade of unnaturally good behaviour. At the same time schoolmasters, magistrates, and vicars would be tuning into the Light Programme with mixed feelings of resignation and trepidation, and workmen across the nation would have refused overtime rather than miss the programme which held the whole of Britain in its grip. For at 6.45 every evening they could hear *Dick Barton – Special Agent*.

This should really be two stories – one about the fictional hero Dick Barton and another about Noël Johnson the young actor who played the role. However, such was the nature of radio in the late 1940s and so great was the success of the programme that there is essentially only one story. Perhaps it was unfortunate for Noël Johnson that, for tens of millions, he *was* radio's 'Special Agent'. Even today, he tells me, that while he is recognized by his appearance as Noël Johnson the actor, he has only to open his mouth and speak for people to say 'Dick Barton!' For three years the two lives – Johnson's real one and Barton's fictional biography – merged into one and then one day in 1949 they separated again.

Dick Barton was born on 10 December 1912 at five o'clock in the afternoon – it was a Tuesday, by the way. The weather had been mild – maximum temperature 52 degrees, minimum 43 degrees – and when our hero first appeared it had just begun to rain. His parents lived in a rented house in High Wycombe and Robert Barton, Dick's father, was senior partner in a flour-milling business but he had started work as an errand-boy in Sheffield. He married Mary Anne Smith from Ealing on the day of George V's Coronation, 22 July 1911, some eighteen months before their only child was born.

Young Dick combined, naturally, the best features of both parents and even at the tender age of two was displaying the kind of gifts that would make him a leader of men. Later, on his first day at the King Edward Grammar School, he went to the rescue of the victim of a bully and then got punished for starting the fight. He 'took the rap' without complaint. He could hardly avoid becoming the hero of the sports field and was captain of the football team for two successive years and went on to study Engineering at Glasgow University graduating in 1933.

A job in the drawing-office of a Liverpool firm lasted twelve months and then Dick applied for a well-paid and adventurous post with a British company who were building an airport in Peru. Two years later saw him in Persia working on the construction of an oil pipe-line and, in the next year, 1937, he was appointed roving maintenance inspector for the International Construction Corporation Limited.

On 10 October 1939 he joined up, and after training at Colchester he was commissioned in the Royal Engineers. Early in 1940 he was sent to France only to be evacuated at Dunkirk where his exploits earned him the Military Cross.

He transferred to Combined Operations in July 1940 and saw service in the Middle East, South-East Asia, and Europe, as a member of No. 20 Commando Unit. By 1945, he had attained the rank of captain and, after demobilization on 5 November of that year, he was still wondering whether to go back to his pre-war job.

Dick Barton was already four years old when Noël Johnson was born on 28 December 1916 in Birmingham. On leaving Bromsgrove School, Worcestershire, he combined an office job with some professional acting but, at the outbreak of war, he joined the Royal Army Service Corps and went to France. Like Barton he was evacuated at Dunkirk but was wounded during the bombing and was forced to spend the next year in an Army hospital before being invalided out in 1941. After a further period of convalescence he returned to the theatre in the autumn of 1941 and resumed a very successful stage career. During this time he met a girl who was working as a set-designer and married her in 1942.

It was in 1944 that he was asked to join the B.B.C. Repertory Company but at first he declined. Early in the following year he was asked again and accepted but after only three months he decided to become freelance again. In 1946 he got his first inkling of the role that was to so dramatically affect his life.

> I'd been doing a six-part radio serial for the B.B.C. Home Service, and after we had recorded the last episode we all went to a pub for a drink. I remember asking Martyn Webster, who had been the producer, what his immediate plans were. It was just a general question but he answered with something about 'being busy with a big new radio serial' and as he said it, he put his finger to his lips as if to say that nobody was supposed to know about it. And that was my first inkling that something was afoot – the something being Dick Barton.

Something *was* afoot and had been ever since Norman Collins took over as Head of the Light Programme on 1 January 1946. There is no reason to believe that he had any thoughts of a 'Special Agent' in his head at that time but he did know that radio serials had a reputation of gaining a large audience. All that had existed so far in B.B.C. history was *The Robinsons* a light-hearted forerunner of *Mrs Dale's Diary* – but Collins had something quite different in mind. In the first written reference to it in the B.B.C. files Collins asked one of his assistants, John McMillan, to investigate the possibilities of a five-day-a-week 'cloak-and-dagger soap-opera'. By July 1946 internal memos were flying round the B.B.C. thick and fast. But one thing at least was certain Noël Johnson would play the lead.

> I never knew whether Martyn Webster had accidentally let out the information about the serial or whether he did it so that I could be in on it but when I asked what it was all about, he looked at me for a moment and then said 'Why? Would you like to be associated with it?' I replied 'What do you think? Work every day!'

Johnson fitted the part perfectly – besides being a very good actor who could grasp a script quicker and read it better than anyone in

the business, he actually *looked* like the fictional hero Bill Barton. Yes, *Bill* was the original name chosen from a list that consisted of Peter Drake, Rex Drake, Peter Fenton, Michael Drake, Peter Grant, Roger Barton, Rex Barton, Pat Barton, Peter Barton, Bill Barton, but *not*, strangely enough, *Dick* Barton. But, as I have said, Johnson looked like Barton – for the fictional hero's appearance had received the same meticulous attention that was to mark every aspect of the Barton saga. Just as the B.B.C. had checked with the Town Clerk of High Wycombe and the Air Ministry in order to find out exactly what the weather was like in the hero's birthplace at 5 p.m. on Tuesday, 10 December 1912, so they had also consulted textbooks on astrology to ascertain exactly what Dick Barton would look like at the age of thirty-five. At this point, the factual story of Barton begins to sound even more bizarre than his fictional adventures.

Meanwhile, the B.B.C. couldn't even find a studio in which to make a trial recording. There was no space in London and Birmingham couldn't oblige. Bristol had the studios but not the staff. One B.B.C. memo concerned with this problem mentions that they were unable to find a secretary or a programme engineer. The recipient had sent the memo back with the simple comment 'This gets worse and worse.' In the end all the problems were resolved and Birmingham agreed to lend its studios for the trial recordings. Norman Collins, back from holiday, had come up with the new name 'Dick Barton' and all that remained to be done was to find the rest of the cast though it was by no means certain at this stage that Noël Johnson would accept the title-role.

At the time, Johnson was acting as anchor man for a radio show called *Music by Melachrino* which went out on Saturday evenings. After one of the broadcasts everybody involved went out to dinner and Noël described what happened.

> We'd just finished dinner and were having a drink when somebody – a stranger to me – came over and said, 'I hear you're going to be our new hero.' I asked him what he meant and he said 'I believe that you're going to play

Dick Barton.' Now at this time I hadn't made up my mind about it and so I said 'Well, there's one or two things that will need to be ironed out before I take it. For a start, I'm not going to just play Barton. I want to do other work – stage work and radio. They haven't got an "exclusive" on me.' At this stage one of my friends kicked me but I didn't know who this stranger was and I ignored the kick and said some more about intending to do other work and added 'And to hell with what the Programme Planner thinks.' Then somebody stopped me and said 'I don't believe you two have met before – Noël this is John McMillan, the Programme Planner.'

Johnson had said that there were one or two things that needed to be ironed out and these were principally money and contract terms. The B.B.C. told him that he would not be paid very much for playing Dick Barton but that if the programme 'took off' and went very well, then they could renegotiate fees. Besides, they said, there would be a lot of money to be made from public appearances, stage work, and commercial exploitation. As for the contract, he would be engaged for three days a week during which time five episodes could be rehearsed and recorded, and he would be free to take on any other radio work that was offered to him. On these conditions, Noël Johnson agreed to take the part and six pilot programmes were recorded in Birmingham.

By general consent they were a great success, but the programme had its critics within the B.B.C., especially among members of the Drama Department. On 14 September 1946 Collins sent a memo to Val Gielgud which began 'I know that you'll hate hearing this but the first instalment of the *Dick Barton* series . . . is really awfully good of its kind and is just what we wanted: on this showing the thing will run for years!' On the bottom of the memo Gielgud had written, 'On the contrary, if you are pleased, so am I.' From Denis Morris, the Midland Region's Programme Director in Birmingham, came another message to Collins. Birmingham was very glad to hear that he had liked the first instalment of *Dick Barton*. 'Several of us', Morris wrote 'have pencilled in our diaries 7 October 1967 for the twenty-first birthday party', and added that they hoped that the ingredients for the party would be more easily available by then.

At 6.45 p.m. on Monday, 7 October 1946, to the accompaniment of 'The Devil's Gallop' by Charles Williams, Dick Barton, Snowy White, and Jean Hunter took the air for the first time (Jock Anderson would not appear until Episode Seventeen). The programme ran for two weeks before the first national newspaper took any notice of it and then, on Saturday, 19 October, the *Daily Worker* announced that the B.B.C. had launched a real dud – '*Dick Barton, Special Agent* – which is so bad as to be almost beyond criticism.' Later, the *Daily Worker*'s Radio Critic managed to tumble to the B.B.C.'s anti-Marxist plot. The villains were invariably foreigners; Snowy and Jock were 'fine ex-service types who know their place as set out in King's Regulations and invariably call their captain "Sir".' This in fact was incorrect. Jock never called Dick either 'Captain' or 'Sir'. If he referred to him at all it was as 'Mr Barton'. Mrs Horrock, Barton's housekeeper, was 'a Tory working women with a heart of gold' and Barton himself, of course, was a 'crypto-Fascist'. So much for the *Daily Worker*.

In December 1946, the correspondence column of *The Times* opened a controversy with a letter headed 'Dick Barton and Prep.' Mrs W. Wright Newsome claimed that 'the poor children grow more concerned from day to day about what Dick Barton and others may do next, than about their own futures or the future of England'. The correspondence to which Johnson himself contributed raged over the Christmas period and on 3 January 1947 Barton had clearly arrived for on that day he was the subject of a *Times* editorial. The serial was favourably compared with the works of Dickens and the whole tone of the leader was encouraging.

Dick Barton with that manly, ringing voice of his [perhaps it would have been fairer to give Johnson the credit for the voice] may not be everyone's idea of a perfect hero, but he must be gratified by the number of voices that have been raised on his behalf. . . . Children are generally rather more tough and sensible than those who fear the influence of serial or cinema are apt to believe, and after all Dick

*Noël Johnson (Dick Barton), Alex McCrindle (Jock), and John Mann (Snowy).*

manages to squeeze his hair-raising adventures into a quarter of an hour – and a quarter of an hour can be a refreshing break in a 'prep' which can often run to six times that length.

The strange thing was that although the serial had been running for less than three months it was already seen as a children's programme and the suggestion had been made that it was harmful. Nöel Johnson told me:

I never went along with this idea that it was harmful to children. What the B.B.C. said to me was that it was 'an experiment – a strip cartoon in sound' and that summed it up very well. It was something completely new in this country and, of course, although it was later to have this colossal juvenile audience it was never intended for children.

You see, Dick Barton was quite normal when the programme started; he smoked, enjoyed a drink, and had a girl-friend, Jean, but gradually all that disappeared. Once the B.B.C. realized that the show had this huge following among children, they became very careful about the script – careful almost to a stupid degree I would say. In my opinion Barton was never harmful even at the beginning. After all, good always triumphed over evil and children could read things much worse in some of the comics that still circulated just after the war.

But the B.B.C. were worried and almost every episode had to be altered in some way or another. For instance, this is what I meant when I said they were careful to a stupid degree: I remember one script which called for the villain to go into a bar for a drink. It had to be altered to a *milk* bar and a glass of milk and so you had this situation where this terrible desperado – who would have happily murdered his own mother for money – went into a milk bar and drank a glass of milk and, of course, Barton had to follow him in. What happened was that Barton had to be superhuman without having any of the magical qualities of a Batman.

One could equally say that Noël Johnson had to be a superstar without any of the advantages of a Sean Connery. The B.B.C. had said that although there would be very little money for playing Dick Barton there would be a great deal to be made from the 'side-effects' in terms of public appearances, stage shows, and commercial exploitation. It is true that Johnson did make a number of appearances, all handsomely paid, as Dick Barton but he felt that these were unsuccessful and soon stopped doing them because the public expected some sort of 'show' or Dick Barton adventure which was clearly impossible. There was a special stage show in Blackpool, intended for one week, called *Strong and Sweet*. In it Johnson – billed as 'Noël Johnson – Radio's Dick Barton' – played a character very much like the famous Special Agent and took up the whole of the second half of the bill. This was to be followed by a fifteen-week music-hall tour for Bernard Delfont with Neil Tuson as Producer.

We had had a special sketch written for the tour but on the Tuesday morning after the Blackpool show had opened Bernie Delfont phoned me and said that he thought we ought to use the same sketch that we had used in Blackpool. I disagreed with him and thought we ought to keep the one that had already been written for the tour. On reflection I think that I was wrong – I think the Blackpool sketch was the stronger of the two. Anyway Bernie said 'It's up to you' and so we used the script that had been written for the tour. The show ran for six weeks and we finally ground to a halt in Folkestone.

As for commercial exploitation, the B.B.C. already had that all tied up. Johnson was offered a very large sum by Kelloggs who wanted to use his signature on their cornflake packets, but he had to refuse. Had he accepted he would have been unable to continue working for the B.B.C. And then there was the film.

Dick Barton was only on the air six months of the year and so it would have been quite easy for Noël Johnson to make a picture but for some reason he wasn't approached.

Probably they thought I didn't look tall enough or tough enough but although I wasn't approached at first, they did ring me up some months later and said that they had had great difficulty in casting it – 'Would you consider playing the lead?' By this time I'd had a chance to think it over and I politely declined, so they finally got Don Stannard to play Barton. I think I was wise to refuse because the picture really was a big 'hoot' – even little children in remote villages laughed all the way through it. It wasn't the actors' fault – the whole point of *Dick Barton* was that it could only be feasible in your mind. It was so 'way out' that if you saw it on the screen your eyes would tell you that it just couldn't happen, but with radio the brain invented its own picture of what was going on. For that reason I don't believe that you could compare it with TV serials like *The Saint* – Barton would just be comedy on television. We always ran through it once at rehearsals just to get rid of the laughs and there really were some big hoots. Strangely enough though there's only one piece of dialogue that has stuck in my mind and it was a classic line. It was the 'curtain line' in one of the pilot programmes and I was with Colonel Gardiner I believe. We all had to rush for the lift and as the door opened Gardiner said 'Great Heavens! There's no floor in the lift!'

The task of writing and producing *Dick Barton* was not an easy one. Daily serials are one of the most demanding forms of radio for a script-writer and for this reason the job is usually undertaken by a team. To avoid any confusion or sudden change of behaviour, the background and nature of the central characters in *Dick Barton* were worked out before the programme ever took the air. And as each new character appeared a file on him would be laboriously built up. Extra special care was taken with Barton himself.

On 20 February 1947 Norman Collins drew up a lengthy memo for the Drama Director and John McMillan. As the series was now being heard by a larger section of the juvenile audience than any other radio programme and as the total audience was probably larger than that for any film or magazine serial, Collins felt that it might be a good thing if they set down certain signposts for the future. Even though Barton was not originally conceived for a juvenile audience 'that' wrote Collins 'is what we have got and we must act accordingly'.

It was simply that the colossal and mounting popularity of *Barton* meant, Collins argued, that they should be aware of 'the really considerable responsibilities which lie upon us as teenage entertainers. Perhaps the easiest way of saying all this is that we should accept the same general standards as those of *The Boy's Own Paper.*'

The memo contained five 'signposts' as Collins called them. They were later elaborated into the twelve 'Rules of Conduct' which appeared on 27 August 1947:

DICK BARTON

RULES OF CONDUCT

1. Barton is intelligent as well as hard-hitting. He relies as much upon brains as upon brawn.
2. He only uses force when normal, peaceful means of reaching a legitimate goal have failed.
3. Barton never commits an offence in the criminal code, no matter how desirable the means may be argued to justify the end.
4. In reasonable circumstances, he may deceive but he never lies.
5. Barton's violence is restricted to clean socks on the jaw. The refinements of unarmed

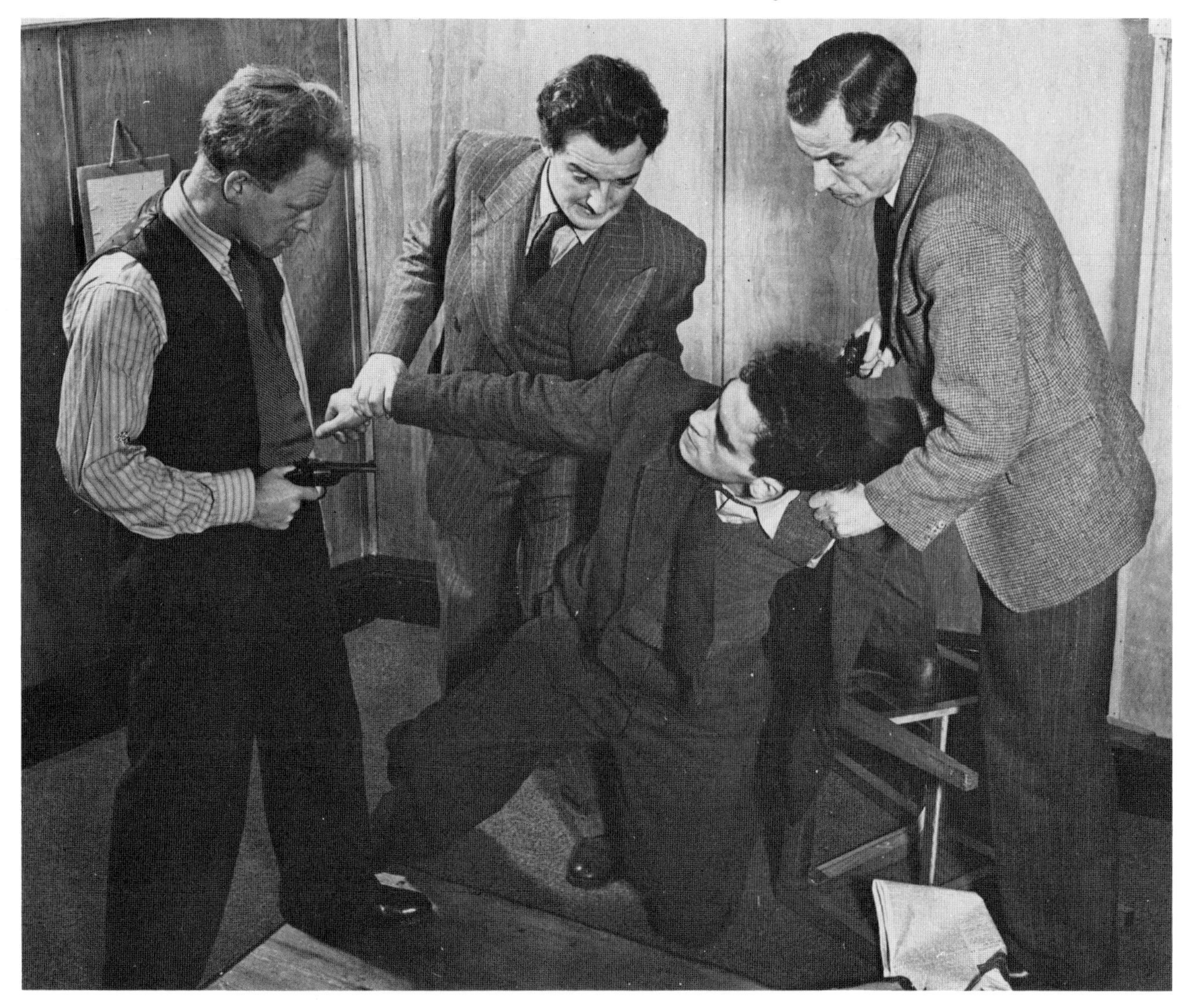

*Normal, peaceful means failed to persuade Limpey played by Alan Tilvern.*

combat taught to British Commandos cannot be practised by him or by his colleagues. When involved in a brawl which ends in victory for the Barton side, he must be equally matched or outnumbered.

6. Barton's enemies have more latitude in their behaviour but they may not indulge in actually giving any injury or punishment which is basically sadistic.
7. Barton and his friends do not wittingly involve innocent members of the public in situations which would cause them to be distressed. For example, a motor car cannot be requisitioned for the purpose of chasing bandits, without the owner's permission.
8. Barton has now given up drink altogether. No reference should be made to its existence in the Barton circle. The villains may drink but never to excess. Drunken scenes are barred.
9. Sex, in the active sense, plays no part in the Barton adventures. In other words, Dick has no flirtations or affairs and his enemies have no molls or mistresses (as opposed to partners). This provision does not of course rule out the possibility of a decent marriage (not involving Dick personally) taking place.
10. Horrific effects in general must be closely watched. Supernatural or pseudo-supernatural sequences are to be avoided – ghosts, night-prowling, gorillas, vampires.
11. Swearing and bad language generally may not be used by any character. This ban ranges from 'bloody' through 'God', 'Damn' and 'hell' to ugly expressions currently heard in certain conversations but not considered admissible for child usage in middle-class homes.
12. Political themes are unpopular as well as being occasionally embarrassing. The-man-who-wants-to-control-the-Earth creates little impact and is best left out of the Barton world.

The Rules of Conduct were just a codified form of the countless memos which passed to and fro. Cuts and alterations to the scripts were frequent – cuts like 'the discussion on Snowy White's morals on page seven because it is faintly smutty', 'I have put a pencil through an exchange between Barton and Gardiner on page three in which Barton poses the question about Miss Hunter's morals', 'I think we should draw the line about using the word "bitch" if applied to a woman', and the general instruction about avoiding the suggestion of sadism – for example, if Barton is 'tied up and flogged we should cut the flogging scene'.

Not only did the script-writers have to contend with the B.B.C.'s sensibilities about drink, swearing, sex, sadism, and almost every other basic ingredient of thrillers, they also had the technical problem of keeping the action going at a cracking pace. It has been authoritatively stated by impartial judges that *Dick Barton* was the fastest radio feature in both Britain and America – fastest in its pace and in its actual production. The speed of production was explained by the fact that everybody involved in the programme were experts at their job and Johnson's ability to master and read a script was legendary. The actual 'pace' of the action was worked out almost mechanically. Each episode had three dramatic peaks. The first was the curtain line of the previous episode. This was carried over from the day before and was disposed of within the first two minutes. Then a new development in the story was started. The usual way to do this was by dialogue but in order to achieve the impression of action, all necessary conversation took place in cars, aeroplanes, or motor launches where the sound-effects could suggest speed. The second dramatic peak would occur in about the sixth minute of transmission and would be followed by the development of a new theme leading up, in the last five minutes, to the major dramatic peak of the episode – the cliffhanger or curtain line. Particular attention was paid to the end of the Friday episode which needed to sustain interest, and excitement, until the next Monday evening.

The plots themselves, although pretty far-fetched in the early days, always had to be completely feasible and incidents in them, such as the dramatic escapes of Dick, Snowy, and Jock, had to be both possible and relatively plausible – *Barton* script-writers were never allowed to resort to the time-honoured device of 'with one gigantic bound our hero was free'. One particular plot idea was criticized – the synthetic iceberg floating in the Atlantic which most people thought a bit improbable. 'In fact,' Noël Johnson told me, 'it was based on an idea that Churchill had during the war.' Apparently several of these 'vessels' were made as supply-bases for anti-submarine forces but before they could be used the need for them had passed.

Despite the meticulous care taken with *Dick Barton* it continued to be the centre of controversy. Opinion seemed equally divided as these headlines show: 'Dick Barton – Too Thrilling for Girls? Headmistress says "Yes"'; 'Dick Barton Does Not Harm Children – School Doctor'; 'Dick Barton – A Parish Decides, Some Say it's Bad, Some Good'; 'At 16 He Prefers G.B.S. to Dick Barton'; 'Another Grandmother Praises Dick Barton'; 'Should Dick Barton Die'; '"I Like Dick Barton," says Mr Morrison'.

On the whole the programme got a favourable Press. If George Bernard Shaw didn't like it, it may have had something to do with the fact that he had never listened to it. Herbert Morrison (then a Minister in the Labour Government) loved it and would allow nothing to interrupt his listening. There was a fear that children, imitating Barton, would become delinquents. But considering that Barton was unable to commit any form of crime or to hit anyone, except when heavily outnumbered by criminals; that he could only then use his fists; that he was forbidden smoking, swearing, drinking, and sex; it seems impossible that an imitator of Dick Barton

LONDON LAUGHS: *By LEE*
"Can Dick Barton outwit the audacious criminals? Will he recover the stolen valuables? Listen again next week..."

*The listener's attention had to be held.*

*Noël Johnson in a public appearance in Birmingham 1948.*

could ever get in any form of trouble.

On the other hand *Dick Barton* was responsible for a number of positive achievements. A fifteen-year-old boy in Cornwall who fell on to a railway track walked away after a train had passed over him. 'I listen to Dick Barton', he said 'and I did exactly what he did when he got under a train – lay flat and kept still.' Another story was headed 'Dick Barton Fan Trailed Crook. Boy Praised in Court'. The boy whose action led to an arrest was eleven years old. There are several stories of this nature and the over-all effect of Barton's influence on the young was probably much greater and *better* than has ever been realized. When a father whose two children were in court for housebreaking tried to lay the blame on Barton, the magistrate sharply replied 'Dick Barton doesn't take other people's property!' Medical Officers, Magistrates, Chief Constables, Directors of Education and Hospital Staff all joined in praising the programme.

Much of the credit must go to the B.B.C. and

the script-writers but it was Noël Johnson who had the task of convincingly putting over this new code of chivalry.

The 'rules' of thriller serials demanded that attention must be centred at all times on the hero. He could have satellites like Jock and Snowy but they existed only to give him someone to talk to and to explain what he was thinking. And the logical development of this was that all the interest, fan worship, and controversy would eventually surround the actor who played the lead.

Johnson had known this all along but what he could not be expected to realize was the actual size of interest that *Dick Barton* would create or that he would have to cope with it single-handedly. Fan-mail was the biggest problem. It belonged to the world of the film star rather than the world that Johnson was used to. Within a few months it had reached the rate of two thousand letters a week which meant that in the period of a six-month radio season Johnson had to spend something like £500 on postage alone – even at the 1940s postal rates. But paying for it wasn't the real problem; it was just physically impossible to answer all the letters. At first the B.B.C. just weren't interested but later Johnson approached them again.

> They asked to see a three-day sample of my mail and so one day I staggered into Broadcasting House with three enormous piles of letters and dropped them all on the reception desk – after that the B.B.C. agreed to handle my correspondence. I told them that I would still supply all the autographs and photographs myself if they'd just type the replies and they said 'All right, we'll do it.'
>
> One day, some months afterwards, I was walking past the Lyric Theatre, where I'd played before, and the stage-doorkeeper came out after me and asked what had happened to me. I asked him what he meant and he told me that his grandniece – I think it was his grandniece – had written for my autograph. And then he showed me the letter that the B.B.C. had sent back. It was about one line of type and said something like 'Thank you for your letter. Mr Noël Johnson regrets that he cannot give any autographs at present.'
>
> I asked if I could borrow the letter but before I went to the B.B.C. about it I took a taxi back to West Hampstead where I was living at the time and got the biggest picture I could find and wrote a message all across it. Then I took a taxi back to the Lyric and said to the doorkeeper 'Please give that to the little girl with my apologies' – then I went to the B.B.C.

Johnson by now was so identified with the role of Dick Barton that he was finding it difficult to get other parts, and although radio producers were anxious to use his services there was a considerable pressure from certain branches of the B.B.C. Administration which managed to discourage any attempt to use the actor who played Dick Barton. Ironically, there were even some people in the B.B.C. Drama Department who were annoyed with Noël for ever accepting the 'Special Agent' role and therefore were reluctant to use him.

Johnson has stressed that he had no quarrel with the B.B.C. who, apart from occasional pieces of heavy-handed bureaucracy – like the case of the stage-doorkeeper's grandniece – were always kind and gracious in their behaviour towards the *Dick Barton* team. 'I don't think that you could find another organization in the world which has this ability to be so gentlemanly and well mannered with the people they employ,' he told me. But the role was – in fact *had* become – his life. People called him Dick; strangers asked him to solve crimes; an old friend who kept a hotel took Johnson aside when he arrived with his wife and said 'Look here, old man, I understand that you're a single man.'

One day in 1949 Noël made a decision which he has never regretted.

I'd been taking part in a radio play with Brenda Bruce and, as she lived in a flat just round the corner from Broadcasting House, she asked me back for a drink during Sunday lunchtime break in rehearsals. As we sat talking I told her that I had had an offer of a stage play. 'But, what about Dick Barton?' she said. I told her that I'd made up my mind to leave. Her late husband Roy Rich was at that time working on the *Daily Express* and while we were talking he had been getting the drinks from the kitchen. Well, when I said this about leaving *Dick Barton*, I heard him drop the ice-tray and then he came in and said 'Does anybody

*Noël stands on a ledge on the roof of Lewis's store in Birmingham to oblige the Press.*

else know? If not, can I have an exclusive?' I told him that nobody knew but that there was already a letter in the post to the B.B.C. and that he could certainly have an exclusive on it. A few days later a reporter came to see me and after an hour he said, 'I can see that there's a story here and I can equally see that I'm not going to get it.' He was right. I never did give the Press the real reason for leaving *Dick Barton* but it was simply money. Later when the B.B.C. asked me to take the role over again I told them how much I would need and they replied 'It sounds to me as if you want danger money.' 'That's *exactly* what I want,' I replied.

Duncan Carse became the new Dick Barton and the programme continued for a couple of years before being replaced by *The Archers* – another product of the *Barton* script-writing team. Noël Johnson went into the stage play *Sweethearts and Wives* and, as he so frankly told me, 'it was a flop'.

It was a long time before he managed to become accepted as an actor again and in the early 1950s he played a role in a radio serial that seemed to confirm that he was type-cast. But 'once bitten twice shy' – this time he insisted that he should play it completely anonymously. And that is why nobody outside the profession ever knew the name of the actor who played the title-role in Radio Luxemburg's *Dan Dare*.

It took a long time for me to be accepted as a straight actor again. Val Gielgud at the B.B.C. had never really approved of my playing the Barton role and I didn't work for him for many years. Then in 1957 I decided to write to him and I said that by now I hoped I had been 'forgiven' for playing Dick Barton. I think I was because he asked me to play the 'Kenny More' part in *The Deep Blue Sea*.

Today he is frequently seen on television and in films (he was recently in Hitchcock's *Frenzy*) and is recognized by viewers as Noël Johnson

*Noël Johnson today.*

the actor. Only occasionally does somebody say 'Wasn't he Dick Barton?' Perhaps it was his sense of humour that made Mr Johnson save a 'cliffhanger' for the end of the interview I had with him recently. Just as he got up to leave he said 'By the way, did you know that the *Dick Barton* rights have been sold to David Frost's television company and that pilot programmes have already been filmed?' And with that curtain line we are left to wait for a possible next episode in the adventures of *Dick Barton – Special Agent*.

# 11. In a Shady Nook

On 24 June 1949 the *News Chronicle* asked the question 'Is Donald Peers a Menace?' Six months before, such a headline would have been unthinkable for few journalists on the National Press, unless they were employed as radio critics, would have known who Donald Peers was.

What was it then that could have prompted a normally sober and respectable national daily to use such a sensational headline? Probably the fact that the Press, like the B.B.C. and the whole of show business, was completely thrown by the success of the man whom the *Sunday Express* had quite rightly called 'The Phenomenon of 1949.'

Donald Peers, one of the most persuasive voices to come out of Wales since David Lloyd George, was born in the mining town of Ammanford and although his mother was Welsh, his parents had met and married in Chicago. It was there that their two eldest children were born. Frank Peers, the singer's father, was a native of Kent who had travelled the world before settling in the United States where he became an evangelist with the Plymouth Brethren. It was at the insistence of his wife's father that they returned to Wales where Mary Peers's family owned and worked on a small newspaper called *Llais Lafur* (The Labour Voice) which had been founded by her father Ebeneezer Rees. And above the printing works was The Coliseum, a small theatre-cum-cinema.

A clever psychiatrist might make something of the fact that Donald Peers could easily have been born and brought up as an American and that his childhood background gave him the combined influences of evangelism, journalism, and the theatre. Certainly these influences were sometimes to be seen at work in his later phenomenal success. No Welsh preacher or American evangelist could have spoken more movingly than he did in his radio series and at his Albert Hall concert; certainly no performer in Britain had ever seen his life so dramatically and happily transformed with the aid of the journalistic profession. And as for the theatre, he was eventually to show a greater mastery of stagecraft than anyone in the business.

Donald's first public performance was at a Sunday School Treat before he was ten. For some time he had been fascinated by an H.M.V. gramophone that belonged to his Uncle David. Although the voices that issued from the horn were metallic and nasal, he considered the whole thing 'miraculous'. He later wrote in his autobiography:

> After many visits, when my good behaviour could be relied on, I was allowed to play records without anybody supervising. There were tenors and contraltos singing arias of all descriptions, choral works and the rest – but the record that appealed to me more than any was one of Billy Williams – 'The Man in the Velvet Suit'. He was singing 'When Father Papered the Parlour'. This in my judgment was nothing less than a masterpiece. I loved

# IN A SHADY NOOK
## BY A BABBLING BROOK

Words by **HARRY PEASE**

Music by **ED. G. NELSON**

*Featured, broadcast & recorded*

*by* DONALD PEERS

PHOTO BY RICHARD CANTOURIS

1/-

*MADE IN ENGLAND*

**KEITH PROWSE & CO. LTD. LONDON, W. 1**

it; played it over and over again and learnt it word for word, note for note.

Soon afterwards the young Donald was asked to contribute a sacred song at the Sunday School Treat. 'Polite applause at the end must have completely turned my head, for I immediately burst into a completely unrehearsed and unsolicited encore and I sang with glee and gusto.' And of course the number he chose was 'When Father Papered the Parlour'.

The faces around him grew sterner with each line he sang and one glance at his father was enough to tell Donald what fate was in store for him when he got home but, already showing signs of being a real 'pro', he carried on to the bitter end in spite of his stony-faced audience – but he avoided singing comic songs at children's parties in the future.

Later Donald won a place at the County Grammar School and despite his growing interest in entertainment, prompted by that ancient gramophone and visits to the projector-room of The Coliseum, it was decided that he should become a teacher. He wasn't very happy with the idea and even the prospect of following his brother Elwyn to the University College of Wales at Aberystwyth couldn't persuade him to view his future with anything except 'loathing and revolt' as he says in his book *Pathway*.

One sunny morning as he sat day dreaming at the back of the class, he happened to suddenly glance up at the face of his teacher. Donald wrote:

> For a moment he was off his guard and he wore an expression of such resigned futility that a thought struck me with almost the physical effect of a blow . . . if I continue and become a schoolmaster I might end up just like that one day. From that moment, however much I might try to disguise it from myself, the future seemed unbearable. . . . I got up and walked out of the room. . . .

His unorthodox exit led to an interview with the Headmaster who listened sympathetically to what young Peers had to say and then caned him and told him to apply himself to his studies. From then on nothing could keep him in that corner of South Wales.

By now the last of his brothers and sisters had left home and one day as he waited at Ammanford Station for the school train he saw two strangers in paint-splashed overalls. Both were in their early twenties and one wore a wide-brimmed stetson, the other a check cap – both at jaunty angles. They had an air about them – they sang as they worked and walked with a swagger. Suddenly young Donald had an idea – he would get a job with these travelling painters who seemed to lead such an interesting and carefree life. By a piece of luck some of the other painters who arrived asked him where they could find digs and Donald was able to fix them up at a neighbour's house. He became friendly with them all and when they left Ammanford they promised to keep in touch. Just before his sixteenth birthday, he got a letter from one of them – Sid Fellowes – telling him that he had found a job for young Peers.

His first job took him all over the country and as he worked, painting Army barracks, he sang. One of his particular favourites was a number he had heard on a Gene Austin record. It was 'Behind the Clouds'. Many years later that same number was to become one of the big hits of his 1949 radio series. But at the time it didn't appeal to Donald's foreman, a Yorkshireman, who said, 'I'd like to hear thee sing a faster kind of song and just keep time with thy brush' – from then on Donald got a lot of practice singing 'Valencia'.

When the painting job eventually finished, Donald's brother, Howell, who was a ship's radio officer persuaded him to join him on the next cruise of the *British Earl* as a mess-room steward. The voyage did him a lot of good by showing him Gibraltar, the Red Sea, the Persian Gulf – places which had previously been merely names on a map, but once home again, Donald resumed his work as a painter – work which took him to the popular seaside resort of Lowestoft.

Ever since he had left home, Donald had spent every possible evening at theatres, music halls, and pier pavilions, so naturally his first thought on arriving at Lowestoft was to search out the local shows. One of the concert parties appearing there was called *Tons of Fun* and its principal comedian was a man named Leonard Morris. One night he bounced on stage with a ukelele and sang a song. 'That', thought Donald, who was one of the show's regular patrons, 'is my line of country' and straight away he went back to his digs and wrote a letter to Morris asking for an audition. Back came a reply by return of post saying that Mr Morris and Mr Newman Maurice (the show's Manager) would indeed be delighted to hear Mr Donald Peers at 11 a.m. on Tuesday and, if satisfactory, a public audition could be arranged for Friday, 9 September. Both went so well that Donald was engaged at £3 a week although, until a solo spot became available, he would have to sing during the interval while the sweets and ices were being served.

The seaside concert party has provided the early training of many a star and certainly a would-be singer still in his teens as Donald was could find no better place to begin a career in show business than the happy and jolly atmosphere of a company like *Tons of Fun*. When the Lowestoft season ended the show went on tour as *Comedy Concoctions*, and thus Donald Peers began the twenty years of travelling up and down the British Isles before he finally became a top-of-the-bill name.

*Comedy Concoctions* didn't last long and throughout the early 1930s Donald was as often out of work as in it. The lowest point was reached in 1932, a year that brought a total of only seven weeks' work, but in April of the following year he secured a date in the B.B.C.'s *Music Hall* programme. It was not his first broadcast; that had taken place when he was still in his teens and he had sung 'In A Shady Nook' for the very first time, but this broadcast of 1933 marked a turning-point in Peers's career for it was the first occasion on which he obtained recognition in the National Press. Collie Knox, probably the most famous radio critic of his day, wrote 'An Appreciation' in the *Daily Express* which began, as many other articles would fourteen years later, with the question 'Who exactly is Donald Peers?' It was quite a long review and Knox described how he had switched on the radio while waiting to go to the theatre. What he heard was a young singer with the same 'knack of phrasing' that had made Bing Crosby a star. He congratulated the B.B.C. on finding this newcomer and said that he saw a personality looming on the radio horizon. It couldn't have come at a better time for Donald who was almost at the end of his tether. The encouragement of the review persuaded him to carry on and it also caused H.M.V. to search him out and give him a recording contract.

As the 1930s progressed, so did Donald's career. He played in theatres all over the country and people began to get to know his signature-tune 'In A Shady Nook'. And he noticed how the audience invariably joined him in that second line 'By a babbling brook'. In 1938 he secured what was to become a record radio contract – eighty-two consecutive weeks on the International Broadcasting Company's Radio Normandie each Sunday. For Donald Peers, who was already topping the bill at some provincial theatres, that black year of 1932 seemed very remote.

His Radio Normandie contract still had twenty weeks to run when, on Sunday, 3 September 1939, Donald tuned in to the B.B.C. to hear Neville Chamberlain declare war.

> My programme was on Normandie at the same time as Chamberlain's broadcast and I was undecided about which to listen to. After a bit of discussion I decided to tune in to the B.B.C. As I listened, I remembered that the song that I opened my programme with was called 'Don't Worry About Me – I'll Get Along'. As it turned out, it was a very appropriate choice.

Donald, like everybody else, joined up and managed to do the occasional B.B.C. broadcast when his Army duties allowed until, in 1944, he was invalided out on D-Day.

That summer he took a holiday in Blackpool only to find himself asked by Jack Taylor to step in as one of the stars of the show at the South Pier where Anona Winn had left to take up other contracts. Donald agreed but said, 'I shall want a lot of money.' 'How much?' Taylor asked. 'A hundred pounds a week', Donald said. Taylor agreed and then asked how much he'd been paid in the Army. 'Eight and ninepence a day', Donald replied.

In October 1945 Donald Peers did a variety tour for Moss Empires – this time as the top-of-the-bill artist and people began predicting that he would be the next big name in British variety. And in 1947 came his first B.B.C. radio series *Cavalier of Song*. It was followed by another in 1948 and Donald was now hovering between being top of the 'Second League' of show business and making the big final breakthrough. He hadn't long to wait for he was engaged for a third radio series to begin on 3 February 1949.

*Donald Peers in 1947.*

That radio series, even today, stands out as one of the great phenomena of British broadcasting. Before it began, the only Press coverage it got was a single paragraph in *The Stage* on 26 January: by early March it was the subject of daily four-column articles in all the national newspapers. Never has a radio programme had such an immediate effect on the public.

There are sound reasons that can be found to explain part of the sudden success, although there will always be questions that just cannot be answered because nobody knows, even given all the information, *exactly* why it happened when it did.

For a start, there was a young Australian called Jim Davidson. He arrived in England in

*Doctors thought a personal visit would help eight year-old Anne Marshall, who had written to Donald asking him to sing to her.*

1948 to take up a job with the B.B.C. and on his first night in this country he and his wife happened to turn on the radio in their hotel room – the programme they heard was *Cavalier of Song*. That first impression of Donald Peers was strengthened when Davidson saw him topping the bill at the Finsbury Empire on the Friday of August Bank Holiday week. Afterwards he went to Donald's dressing-room and told him how he had been impressed by the way he had established contact with the audience – 'that's how I want to present you over the air' he announced. Two years later, to the very day, Jim Davidson sat in a theatre and saw Donald topping the bill again, only this time it was the London Palladium.

Davidson's idea about broadcasting Donald with an audience had occurred to the singer himself at the time of the first series but it was not B.B.C. policy to give studio audiences to solo singers. Now, however, they relented and promised Donald a studio audience in 1949.

Another factor was that during the previous series the Producer, Roy Speer had suggested that Donald should write the link-ups between the songs and read them himself in place of the announcer. It seemed a good idea and he spent several hours each week on preparing a six-minute script. Read 'cold' over the air they sounded well written but that was all. But when in 1949 Donald delivered them to his studio audience they went a long way towards producing the atmosphere of sincerity that characterized the series. And, of course, by the time 1949 arrived Donald had gathered round him some of the finest talents in the business. There was Wally Ridley who had worked closely with Vera Lynn, Roy Speer the Producer and, especially brought in for the first programmes of the series, the Conductor, Charles Shadwell. With all these good omens it was obvious that the 1949 *Cavalier of Song* series would be the best so far.

A small note in *The Stage* on 26 January 1949 announced that 'a new weekly series of programmes by "The Cavalier of Song" Donald Peers' would commence on 3 February and that they would be broadcast from the stage of the Kilburn Empire. After that *The Stage* got rather left behind by the national dailies who got to hear of 'strange happenings' at these Sunday-night shows. In an interview Mr Peers told me:

> I'd learnt all special songs for the first show and after the recording of the broadcast the audience literally stood their ground. So with my pianist and drummer, I gave them another half hour's singing. We all had a wonderful time and at the end of that half hour they came storming up on to the stage. The second week was really quite outrageous and by the time the third programme was recorded the Press were there in force.

Meanwhile the B.B.C. awarded him, what was at the time, their biggest one-man contract ever – for fifty-two consecutive weeks. The story appeared in the *Daily Mirror* on 5 March, two days after Collie Knox had mentioned the show in the *Daily Mail*. On 7 March several national dailies including the *Mirror* and *Herald* gave the programme front- and inside-page coverage. On 8 March the *Evening Standard* sent their 'Casebook' reporter to see him. The *Yorkshire Evening News* ran a two-column story on 9 March, and then the South Wales papers took up the story of Donald Peers. So did the Australian Press where the *Sydney Sun* ran a special story. In Britain *Illustrated* and *Picture Post* also prepared 'specials' while both *Life* and

*When Donald appeared in Cardiff in 1949, he employed this disguise to escape frenzied fans who had stripped him of his clothes on the previous night.*

*Time* magazines sent reporters and photographers to Donald's recording session. After mid March, however, it became impossible to keep up with the flood of newspaper articles about the show.

'Women Mob Radio's Cavalier of Song: B.B.C. is Bewildered', said the *Daily Herald*; 'The Girls, They'd Clean His Shoes', claimed a *Daily Mirror* headline, both reports appeared on 7 March. The *Daily Herald* report said:

> Women cried out, Girls screamed 'Oh Donald! *Donald*!' in fantastic hero-worship at Hammersmith last night. . . . B.B.C. officials were bewildered. Producer Roy Speer scratched his head and said 'I've never known anything like it' and was jostled away by the surging crowd. After each song there was bedlam from all over the theatre and youngsters yelled 'More! Give us more Donald!' Then came the remarkable reception at the stage door.

Donald seemed to be as genuinely bewildered as everybody else and told the Press that, although it was all very nice, he just couldn't understand why it should suddenly be happening to him. The public went wild with delight and self-congratulation in finding a hero who was not only talented but also so modest and level-headed.

A small number of people, however, began to darkly hint that all was not what it seemed. 'You know what he's done don't you?' they whispered. 'He's hired Frank Sinatra's Press agents.' Actually it wasn't true – Donald's only Press agents were the fans themselves whose behaviour invited reporting. Donald himself, although he had built up a reputation in the provinces, knew absolutely no one on the London Press except Collie Knox to whom he had written only once, fourteen years previously.

In May 1949 came the great moment that overshadowed all the later triumphs, even that of starring at the London Palladium, for on the ninth of that month Donald Peers single-handedly gave a two and a half hour show at the Royal Albert Hall. It was the first time any variety artist had attempted such a thing. Five thousand people were expected, nearly nine thousand were in the hall when the show began. From the moment that he signalled his pianists Joe Henderson and Ernest Ponticelli to play his signature-tune, he could do no wrong. The next day the concert made front-page news in all the papers. Eve Perrick summed it up best with one headline which read 'The Babbling Brook Floods the Albert Hall'. Donald rather liked that one.

The Albert Hall concert was a strange mixture of adulation and seaside jollity and Donald knew exactly how to balance the two. He began by quoting something Ruskin had said about beginning at the beginning and ending at the end – it was another way of saying that he would start with 'In A Shady Nook'. 'If I can make you happy in any way', he told them, 'but especially by singing, then I feel that I've served some purpose.' But he not only sang himself, he let the audience sing to him, knowing like all artists with their roots in seaside concert-parties, that the British public are always prepared to pay good money to entertain themselves. And at the end of the evening as the last notes of his signature-tune died away he disappeared under a scrimmage of fans who hurled themselves at the dais.

All this sort of thing slightly worried the Press who wondered whether the fan-worship was becoming dangerous. Hence that headline in the *News Chronicle* 'Is Donald Peers a Menace?' Underneath a sub-heading ran, almost with an editorial sigh of relief, 'on the contrary, says psychiatrist'.

The *News Chronicle* sent the psychiatrist to Blackpool where Donald was now starring in a summer show. After seeing the show the psychiatrist was asked the following questions: (1) Why was Donald Peers such a success? 'Because he has developed a special microphone technique and because he is sincere.' (2) Why does he appeal to the older generation? 'Because he is homely and sings the songs of the older generation.' (3) Why does he appeal to the teenagers? 'Because he sings popular songs like "Lavender Blue" – songs with rhythm.' As one girl said, 'You feel he is singing to you'. (4) Why do teenage girls swoon when Peers sings? 'I think that it is the reaction of emotional young adults. I think the stories of girls going into trances may quite easily be true.' (5) Do you think that Peers's singing has an unhealthy effect on young girls? 'There is very little sex about it, if any at all.' (6) Do you think Peers is a good or bad thing for the country? 'Good. He is helping to keep the



*After the Albert Hall concert.*

people's spirits up. He even makes them sing in their own homes when they are listening to him on the radio.'

The assessment was a pretty fair one. Peers did manage to appeal to all age groups and he was sincere. Certainly he did have a good effect on the people who listened to him. In an interview with the author Mr Peers said:

> In those days everybody had been singing nothing but slow songs. I picked the songs that they wanted to hear – songs that had been there all the time but that nobody had sung. I told them that life wasn't so bad after all – and it paid off.

There were songs like 'Powder Your Face With Sunshine', 'Behind the Clouds', and many more 'cheer-up songs' as Donald called them. These certainly had the right effect but there was something else. The *News Chronicle*'s psychiatrist had said that there was little, if any, sex involved in the fan-worship of Peers. But there was an incredible emotional atmosphere that came over powerfully in recordings of the radio programme.

*The Evening News*

*"Clever of you to fix our Women's Rally for Wednesday, 7.30 p.m. . . . Donald Peers' time!"*

Nowhere is this more apparent than in the last show of the 1949 series. The feeling is similar to that of a particularly highly charged revivalist meeting and the whole of the second half of the programme consisted of Donald's farewell.

'I've always maintained', Donald says on the recording, 'that when the time comes to say goodbye, we should do so quickly. Thank you for *all* that *you* have *meant* to me. I hope my *song* will *linger* in your memory [pause] for you will always live in my heart.' It was delivered slowly and in that emotional voice that so many millions had listened to with bated breath every week. As he spoke there were loud murmurs from the audience and Donald himself sounded genuinely overcome by the drama and emotion of the occasion. When he finished, pandemonium broke loose – they screamed, they cried, and they begged him to stay and as they did so the orchestra played 'In a shady nook, By a babbling brook', and gradually the audience joined in. When it came to the last verse, Donald sang three lines himself, 'By a babbling brook, that's where I fell in love with you'. And then the orchestra played it again and again and the audience cried 'Donald! *Donald*!' The whole thing was both outrageous and very moving at the same time and anyone hearing that recording must still wonder *what* exactly caused that incredible reaction to happen for the first time.

Later in 1949 Donald was forbidden to sing by his doctors. He had an operation and was out

*Donald leaves for Australia, 1954.*

*Donald Peers today.*

of action for a year. When he came back he topped the bill at the London Palladium, the first British male singer to do so for many years. And for the next four years he remained the most popular singer in Britain.

In 1954 he went to Australia where his records had been outselling everyone else's for some time. He stayed for two years and when he returned in 1956, a new sound was all the rage – rock 'n roll. Theatres were closing all over the country because of television, and it seemed that the music hall was finally dead. Donald Peers had to virtually start all over again.

'I took a long hard look at show business', he wrote, 'and decided that entertainment wouldn't stop and that the music-hall audience would appear somewhere else.' In 1958 he found that audience again in the Northern Clubs and became the first star name to work in them. Today the clubs are one of the highest paid media for entertainers and as I write Donald Peers is once again in the charts with his latest record and starring in variety shows as he has always done – but this time on television.

# 12. Raising the Laughs

FOR THE TENTH YEAR

Mr. Thomas Handley

*This Evening begs to Present his Celebrated Extravaganza*

ITMA

By Mr. Edward Kavanagh

The following well-known artists have consented to appear:

MR. JOHN TRAIN MR. MORTON MR. FREDERICK YULE

MR. D. GUYLER MISS DIANA MORRISON

MISS JOAN HARBEN and MISS HATTIE JACQUES

*ALSO*

A Glee Party directed by Mr. George Mitchell

*AND*

The Orchestra conducted by Mr. Jenkins

THE ENTIRE PRODUCTION under the supervision of MR. WORSLEY

*TONIGHT AT 8.30*



*From the* Radio Times.

After the war, *ITMA* still dominated the comedy scene and Tommy Handley's adventures as Governor of the newly discovered island of Tomtopia were followed just as avidly as all his previous ones had ever been. It had been decided in 1945 that with the end of the war, the time had come to change some of the old faces – or voices – before the listeners got bored. And so such characters as Signor So-So, Mrs Mopp, Sam Scram, the Diver, and many others were dropped from the team. The change of locale was easily effected for on the first show of the 1945–46 series a messenger informed Tommy that His Majesty's Government requested that he leave the realm immediately to take up an appointment as a colonial governor.

In Tomtopia Handley discovered a whole host of new characters. There was the two-faced Welshman, Sam Fairfechan (Hugh Morton) and Major Munday (Carleton Hobbes) who, it turned out, was an old friend of Colonel Chinstrap. Munday had a daughter Naive (Jean Capra) who was always asking simple questions that Tommy found so difficult to answer. And then there was Big Chief Bigga Banga (Fred Yule), his daughter Banjoleo (Lind Joyce), and a public-school-educated native called Wamba M'Boojah (Hugh Morton).

As series followed series many more characters were introduced and the locale changed frequently. Deryck Guyler created Frisby Dyke and Molly Weir played Tattie Mackintosh. It seemed that there was no limit to the comic inventions that Handley, Kavanagh, and Worsley could provide and on 28 October 1948 *ITMA* celebrated its 300th edition – it was its tenth year.

In this particular programme, Tommy was a resident in Henery Hall, a home for tramps run by Matron Hotchkiss and the show looked back

*Tommy Handley in America, 1947.*

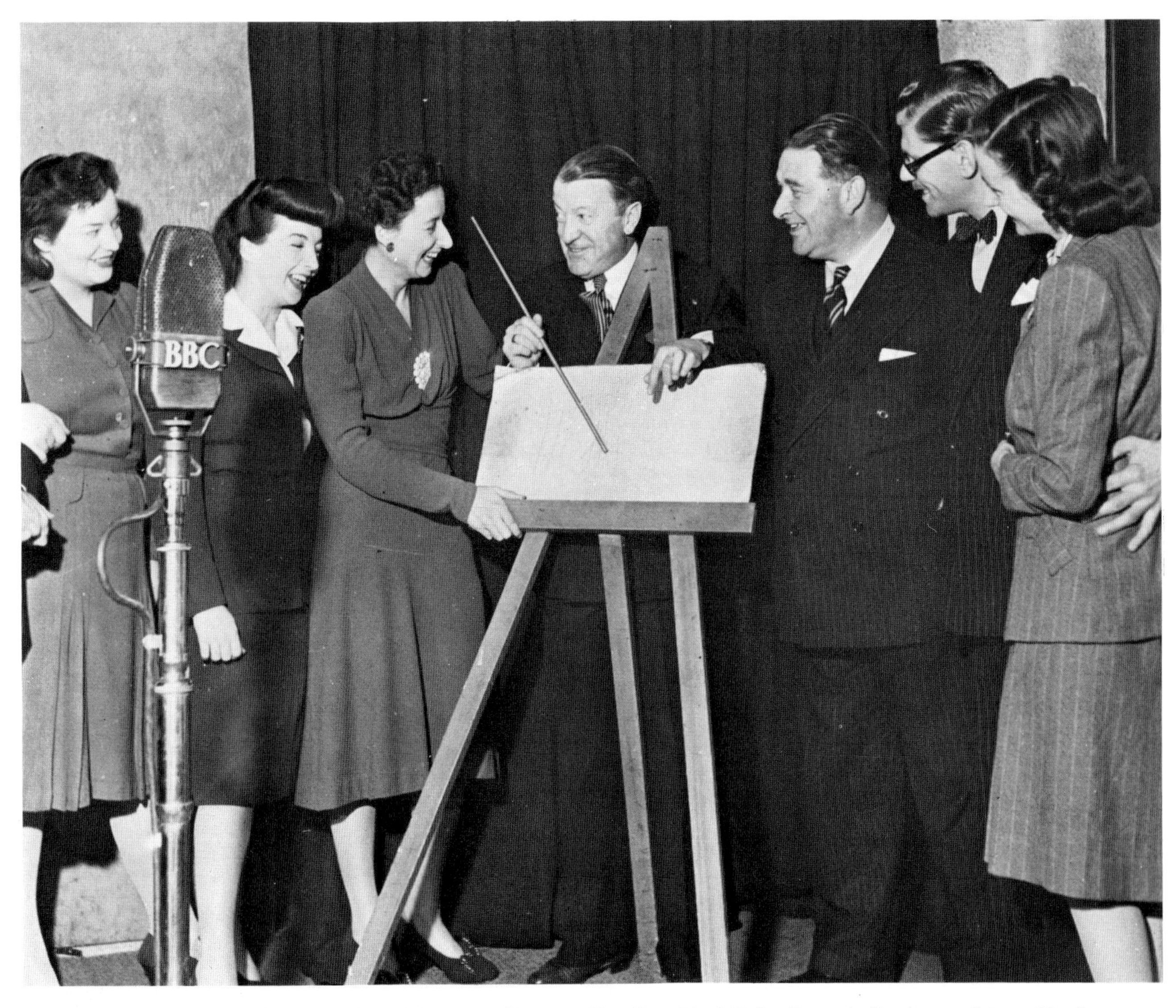


*Hattie Jacques, Lind Joyce, Diana Morrison, Tommy Handley, Fred Yule, Deryck Guyler, and Joan Harben.*

on its past achievements. All the old characters made brief appearances and it was a great occasion for both the listeners and the *ITMA* team.

On 5 January 1949 came the 310th edition of the show and in it Tommy was to become Manager of Uncle Tom's Cabin – a coffee-stall. In the programme with him were Mona Lott (Joan Harben), Frisby Dyke (Deryck Guyler), and Sophie Tuckshop (Hattie Jacques). It had been intended that the coffee-stall would give Tommy the basis of a new series of adventures but in fact this would be the last edition of *ITMA* for, a few days later, on the afternoon of 9 January 1949, Tommy Handley died in a private nursing-home after suffering a cerebral haemorrhage in his flat.

At his funeral, they lined the streets six deep,

for six miles and 10,000 people waited at the crematorium. Thousands more waited outside St Paul's later when the Memorial Service was held. No British entertainer has ever been paid such a tribute and the B.B.C., recognizing the unique role that Handley had played, wisely decided that *ITMA* should die with him. So ended one of the most loved shows in the annals of British broadcasting. During its ten-year run it had brought laughter to millions, not only in war but equally in peace. And its creators had given the public more comic characters and catch-phrases than anyone since Charles Dickens.

With the death of Tommy Handley the B.B.C. was presented with a difficult problem. Having wisely decided to let *ITMA* die with its star, it

*Outside St Paul's on the day of Tommy's Memorial Service.*

was now faced with the loss of its top comedy show.

There was no shortage of claimants for the *ITMA* crown. Charlie Chester's *Stand Easy*, Murdoch and Horne's *Much Binding in the Marsh*, and Eric Barker's *Waterlogged Spa* all enjoyed enormous popularity but the real beneficiary of the *ITMA* legacy was a show called *Take It From Here* which had been languishing in the programme schedules since it first took the air on 23 March 1948.

Of its three stars, only Australian Dick Bentley had any extensive history in 'the business'. He had come to England in 1938 and been spotted by a B.B.C. Producer when singing in a night-club. After touring with the Australian Forces during the war he returned to this country in 1947 and met his future co-stars while broad-

*Dick Bentley, Joy Nichols, and Jimmy Edwards.*

casting in an edition of *Navy Mixture* – a revamped war-time show in which Jimmy Edwards and Joy Nichols were then the resident artists.

Jimmy Edwards was a recent, and unlikely, recruit to show business. Educated at St Paul's Cathedral Choir School and King's College School, Wimbledon, he won a singer's scholarship to St John's College, Cambridge, where he gained his M.A. degree.

The war saw him as Flight-Lieutenant Edwards, D.F.C., and in late 1944 he was shot down over Holland and spent several months in the 'burns' ward of an R.A.F. hospital in Ely.

In 1945 Edwards went into show business by 'luck coupled with my natural laziness and inclination to drift' as he wrote in his book *Take It From Me*. With a background of Cambridge *Footlights* revues and a number of R.A.F. camp concerts, Edwards sought out Sid Fields's agent who sent someone to see him perform and arranged an audition for Jim at the Windmill Theatre.

Although Van Damm at the Windmill told Edwards that the only funny thing in his act was his moustache, he gave him a contract to start work there in a few weeks' time on 20 May 1946. The salary was £25 a week which, at the rate of six houses a day, six days a week, worked out at the princely sum of approximately 13*s*. 11*d*. per show.

At the Windmill, Edwards developed a technique of insulting the audience which he considered to be highly effective. 'No matter how insulting I became, no one ever answered me back' he wrote and concluded that perhaps this could be explained by the audience's desire not to be recognized. Even in these early days, Edwards had developed all the props of his act; the mortar-board was there and so was the trombone which he played exceptionally well.

After nearly a year and a half at the Windmill, Edwards became involved in a difference of opinion with Van Damm, the proprietor. He had introduced a rule that all performers should be at the theatre half an hour before the first show began and provided a book for them to sign to prove they were there. Perhaps not surprisingly, Edwards flatly refused to comply with the new rule and reluctantly Van Damm gave him the sack.

Just before this happened, Edwards had managed to land a regular spot in the B.B.C.'s revival of the war-time show *Navy Mixture* which also included a young Australian singer called Joy Nichols. At first the two residents of the show took an instant dislike to one another but soon they became firm friends.

When that series of *Navy Mixture* ended its Producer, Charles Maxwell got together with Frank Muir (who wrote Edwards's material) and Denis Norden and they came up with the idea of a show that would include Jimmy, Joy, and Joy's fellow Australian, Dick Bentley, who had been a popular guest artist in *Navy Mixture*.

The first *Take It From Here*, for that was the name of the new show, was broadcast on 23 March 1948, Edwards's birthday, and despite its low audience figures, its initial six-week run was extended, chiefly, Edwards believed, because as three young and relatively little-known broadcasters, the show's stars were very cheap.

By January 1949 the show had developed into a much slicker, fast-paced vehicle for its trio who had by now been joined by Wallis Eaton with his plaintive cry of 'Come 'ome, Jim Edwards.' On 9 January the *Take It From Here* team were rehearsing at the Paris Cinema for the current week's show when Tommy Handley died. The B.B.C. had now to fill space left by *ITMA* which had given three repeats a week and it was decided to fill one of the vacant half-hours – the Saturday lunch-time 'spot' – with *Take It From Here*.

Fortunately for all concerned, that particular edition of the programme was a very good one and its new audience were pleased with it. From then on the listening figures went up and the radio critics began to hail *Take It From Here* as *ITMA*'s successor.

The programme was, for its time, quite satirical and its sophisticated approach made its success all the more surprising to the B.B.C. and the critics. It was mainly a young team which helped, of course, and it was the first major show for both artists and writers. Frank Muir and Denis Norden, in fact, wrote the show backwards, starting with the last item, usually a burlesque of a film, then writing what they called 'the gimmick' which was a satirical skit on a current news item, and finally they wrote the opening of the programme which always consisted of Dick, Joy, and Jimmy doing a gag routine about something that had happened to one of them. By this method it was possible to include a topical incident with which to open the show.

*Take It From Here* rapidly grew in popularity and to the surprise of all involved in its production it won the *Daily Mail*'s National Radio Award as the best show of 1949. The following year, 1950, a new show, *Educating Archie*, got the nomination but in 1951 *Take It From Here* won the award again after narrowly beating *Life With the Lyons*.

The early 1950s saw the appearance in the show of the Glums. Many people see them as the watershed in B.B.C. comedy. Certainly at the time they represented a wholly new departure in public taste. The boorish loud-mouthed Mr Glum played by Jimmy Edwards – who else? – was quite different from the stock characters of radio comedy. His son Ron was played by Dick Bentley and Ron's fiancée Eth was June Whitfield, who incidentally must be the greatest supporting actress in the history of B.B.C. comedy.

'Oh Ron', . . . 'Yes, Eth?'; this exchange was one of the classic lines of *Take It From Here* and while Eth tried to arouse Ron's interest in getting married or getting a job or in virtually anything, Mr Glum would be outside the door waiting to burst in at the most inopportune moment, to seize on a piece of conversation and lewdly misconstrue it.

It was all refreshingly new and immensely popular and the Glum family stand out as one of the truly great and memorable comedy creations of British radio. Ron, Eth, and Mr Glum remained in the programme until its last broadcast on 3 March 1960.

Just over a year after *Take It From Here* began, a new comedy show took the air. *Ray's A Laugh*, first heard on 4 April 1949, starred, of course, Ted Ray who had broadcast for the first time ten years previously.

Charlie Olden sometime Nedlo, the Gypsy Violinist, and for the last forty-odd years Ted Ray, was born in Wigan. His father was a touring character comedian who called himself Charlie Alden – the family name, however, was Olden. He was a first-class mimic and singer and was very much in demand, but soon after Ted's birth he was persuaded by his wife to settle down and take a pub.

When Ted, or Charlie Olden, was quite young, his family moved to Liverpool where he managed to win a free place at the Liverpool Collegiate School.

Like his father and his father before him, Charlie Olden junior learnt to play the violin –

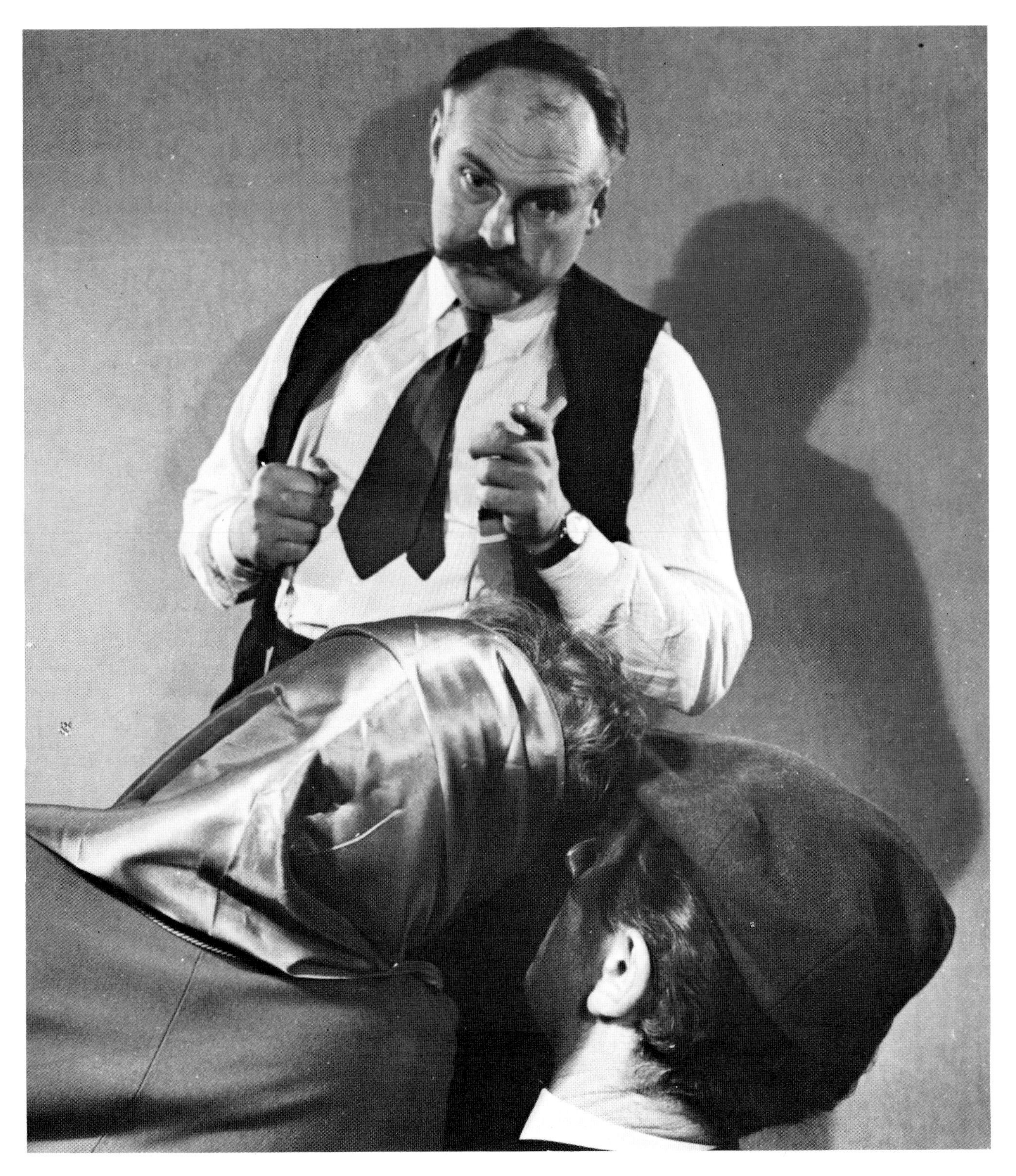

*Mr Glum (Jimmy Edwards) gives some fatherly advice to Ron (Dick Bentley) and Eth (June Whitfield).*

his mother paid 1*s*. 6*d*. a week for his lessons but neither he nor his parents had any thoughts about a career in show business for the future Ted Ray. He once said that his ambition as a child was either to be a cowboy or Prince of Wales but his father compromised and got him an office job with a cattle-food manufacturer. It was the first of many jobs and during one of his early periods of unemployment he was spotted playing football by a scout for Liverpool Football Club and signed for the junior team, Ainsdale Football Club with whom he stayed for two seasons.

In 1926 he made a trip to America as a ship's steward and on his return managed to get a job as a violinist in a dance band. A double act, Wardle and Olden, followed and then Ted became a solo act singing parodies of popular songs and playing the fiddle under the name of 'Hugh Neek'. He worked almost entirely in cinemas and it was in one of these that an agent E. C. Jazon, who had gone in for a sleep, spotted Ted and signed him up under the new name of 'Nedlo the Gypsy Violinist'.

He toured in a number of revues before finding himself back in Liverpool and once again out of work. Jazon had told him that he should stick to playing the violin and doing a few dance steps but that under no circumstances should he open his mouth.

After a few attempts as a stand-up comic, Ted began to think Jazon was right until suddenly, after returning by train from a particularly disastrous engagement, a thought struck him. As he wrote in his autobiography, *Raising the Laughs*, 'I found myself thinking – You've been wrong all along. Why keep yourself aloof from the audience? Why not be *one* of them? Forget all the comic make-up, the white bowler-hat, these fantastic, ridiculous "props". Why, there's no need even to bother about a dinner-jacket. Just be human. Stroll on to that stage in an ordinary suit, just as if you'd walked in out of the street.'

He put his new theory to the test at his next engagement and was an immediate success with the audience. But it was no 'fame in a night' story. Work was still difficult to come by but he had a lucky break and managed to get a booking at the London Music Hall in Shoreditch in May 1930. Again he was a great success with the audience and was sought out by the agent George Barclay who signed him up, but asked him to change his billing from Nedlo. After running through the names of various golfers, they came up with 'Ted Ray', and thus began a new chapter in the story of Charlie Olden.

A tour of South Africa followed and back in England Ted Ray toured in a show headed by G. H. Elliot and Gertie Gitana. And then in 1932 he appeared on the bill at the London Palladium.

The years of struggle were behind him and from then on his career took an upward turn. On 11 July 1933 he married Sybil Stevens at Croydon Registry Office.

It was not until 1939 that Ted Ray made his first broadcast in the B.B.C.'s *Music Hall*. His act went over quite well *twice* for, although the live transmission went on the air, the recording machines had broken down and when they were repaired he had to repeat all his gags again before the same studio audience.

Later in 1939 the B.B.C. had the idea of doing a programme which would feature 'a Crazy Gang of the Air'. It was called *Just Fooling* and starred Binnie Hale, Dave and Joe O'Gorman, and Ted Ray. The first edition of the programme was judged to be a great success and Ray looked forward to a long run but, before the second show

*Ted Ray in a 1940 stage show.*

could be broadcast, war broke out and the series was dropped. It was ten years before the chance came again.

When, in 1949, the B.B.C. did finally get round to giving him a series, Ted Ray had 'arrived' as one of Britain's top comedy stars and the show *Ray's A Laugh*, which was first broadcast on 4 April 1949, quickly established itself as a favourite with the listeners.

It was mainly a domestic comedy although it did include such features as 'George, the Man with a Conscience' in which George, played by Ted Ray was continually at odds with the voice of his conscience, supplied by Leslie Perrins. But, as I said, it was mainly a domestic comedy featuring Ted and his 'radio wife', the Australian Kitty Bluett. Nelson, Ted's brother-in-law, was played by Fred Yule – a recruit from *ITMA* –

*Kitty Bluett, Ted Ray, Kenneth Connor and producer Leslie Bridgmont with the* Ray's A Laugh *team.*

although later the role would be taken over by Kenneth Connor and a variety of voices and characters were supplied by a twenty-three-year-old impressionist called Peter Sellers.

Music was supplied by Stanley Black and the B.B.C. Dance Orchestra and by Bob and Alf Pearson and later a young singer called John Hanson was introduced into the show. From the ranks of the Third Programme, Ray chose Patricia Hayes who played, among other roles, Crystal Jollybottom and said 'Stop it, you saucebox!', and also from 'the Third' he picked Charles Leno who played 'Dear old Dad' who had 'lost his faith in human nature'. And another addition to the cast, for the third series, was Graham Stark. Altogether it was a very gifted team.

It had its catch-phrases, of course, and its

greatest one occurred in the exchange between Ivy (Ted Ray) and Mrs Hoskin (Bob Pearson). 'I've sent for young Dr Hardcastle', said Mrs Hoskin to which Ivy replied 'He's loo-vely Mrs Hoskin . . . he's loo . . . ooo . . . vely!' And like many of the characters in *Ray's A Laugh* Ivy and Mrs Hoskin did exist in real life – Ted and his wife met them on holiday – and never missed hearing themselves impersonated on the programme. There were other catch-phrases – some caught on – 'If you haven't been to Manchester, you haven't lived' did and so did 'It was agony, Ivy', but 'What about the Rovers!' didn't for some reason.

For a time Ted Ray starred not only in *Ray's A Laugh* which occupied the old *ITMA* spot on Thursdays but also in *Calling All Forces*. He also starred in several films including the 'Red Peppers' story in *Meet Me Tonight*.

*Ray's A Laugh* was broadcast for the last time on 13 January 1961 but Ted is regularly seen on television in *Jokers Wild* where his ability as a quick-fire gag-man is seen to its best advantage. The other resident of *Jokers Wild* is Arthur Askey and Ted also appears in a radio programme called *Does the Team Think* with Jimmy Edwards, which all goes to prove something about the staying power of wireless stars.

BBC

# 13. We're Educating Archie

One of the most unlikely shows ever to be heard on the wireless was Peter Brough's *Educating Archie*, which was broadcast for the first time on 6 June 1950.

The very idea of a ventriloquist's act on radio was clearly absurd yet Edgar Bergen with his dummy 'Charlie McCarthy' had been doing the same thing in America since the 1930s. And when Peter Brough did finally manage to persuade the B.B.C. to give him his own show, 'Archie Andrews' suddenly became one of the most successful names in British show business.

Peter Brough was born in Ealing in 1916, the son of a ventriloquist who, under the billing of 'Arthur Brough and Tim' topped the bills at most of the first-rank music halls in the country. Peter's father combined his theatrical life with working in the textile business and when in 1922 his health gave way, he was forced to choose between his two careers. Sir Oswald Stoll, head of the vaudeville theatre circuit, offered him a five-year contract but Arthur Brough, realizing the difficult times that were ahead for music-hall artists, decided to give up the stage.

Some ten years later when Peter had left school and was working at Selfridges Arthur Brough received a letter thanking him for appearing in a concert. At first he was puzzled but then he realized that the letter was intended for Peter. Naturally he was pleased that his son was carrying on the tradition – for Arthur Brough's own father had also been a ventriloquist – but he insisted on two things. First, that Peter should only take it up if he was prepared to work hard at perfecting his art and second, that he should always have a second string to his bow and never be wholly dependent on show business for a living.

Peter Brough went through the 1930s appearing at Masonic dinners and concerts until in 1938 he secured his first B.B.C. audition with Ernest Longstaffe. Afterwards Longstaffe was very charming but made no secret of his opinion that there was no future in sound broadcasting for an amateur ventriloquist.

On the other hand, Peter's other career was going well. Although he was only twenty-three he was already running his own textile agency when war broke out. In 1940 he joined the R.A.S.C. and, naturally enough, got involved in organizing Army concerts. Captain George Black – of the theatre chain – saw Brough doing his act and arranged to have him transferred to one of the 'Stars in Battledress' units where he met such figures as Charlie Chester, Alec Pleon, Nat Gonella, and Donald Peers. But a chest ailment soon caused him to be invalided out.

Back in civilian life Brough came in contact with Wally Ridley, a music-publisher – the man who had been associated with Vera Lynn's radio career and would later play an important part in Donald Peers's phenomenal success. He had seen Brough go through his act at Golders Green Hippodrome and after the show he said 'Your act is old fashioned – your patter is weak. And your dummy – that's atrocious! If you're prepared to get down to work and start again from the beginning, you stand a chance because the raw material is there. If not, then you'll never rise far above the "wines and spirits" on any Variety bill!'

It was brutal advice but Brough was only twenty-eight and he had enough time to start again. And Wally Ridley promised to help. Brough was still in the textile industry and so he invited Ridley to join him on a business trip to Scotland where they spent a week trying out new voices.

Suddenly one seemed to click. It was the treble voice of a fourteen-year-old boy. The next job was to draw a face, which Brough did and took it to George Davenport who owned a magical shop in New Oxford Street, to make a three-dimensional model of the head. From four papiermâché masks, Brough chose the one which was to form the basis of the dummy. All that was needed now was a name and it was supplied by Ted Kavanagh, the famous script-writer of *ITMA*. He took one look at the dummy and said, 'The name, Peter, is Archie Andrews.'

Archie Andrews existed all right but the problem was to get him before the public. As Brough later wrote in 1955, 'Once more my thoughts turned to radio, then as now, the open sesame to success in all other spheres of the entertainment world.' So another audition was arranged – this time with John Sharman, creator and producer of the B.B.C.'s *Music Hall.*

This time it was a success and Sharman booked Brough *and* Archie Andrews for his programme. About the same time the act was booked for a music-hall tour which brought Archie and Peter into contact with stars like Joe Loss, Max Miller, Bud Flanagan and Chesney Allen, Wee Georgie Wood, Robb Wilton, Nervo and Knox, Naughton and Gold, 'Monsewer' Eddie Gray, and many others. Meanwhile, a year elapsed between the first broadcast with Archie and the next piece of radio work, which was a spot in the war-time version of *Navy Mixture*.

The act proved so popular that the Producer, Charles Maxwell offered Brough a regular item in the programme and called it 'Archie Takes the Helm'. The script was written by Ted Kavanagh and Sid Colin, the writer of *Hi Gang* and *Ignorance Is Bliss*, and it gained quite a substantial reputation for Archie and Brough.

After the *Navy Mixture* series finished the new act was booked for many music-hall dates and guest appearances in B.B.C. shows but what Peter Brough always wanted was his own series just like Edgar Bergen's in America. So with the help of Wally Ridley and script-writer Sid Colin, he set to work to sell the idea to the B.B.C.

The plan was for an 'Archie Andrews Radio

Show' which would include film star Bonar Colleano and wireless comedian Jon Pertwee in its cast and a trial recording was made. Tommy Handley, Kenneth Horne, and Ted Kavanagh turned up to wish Brough well and the sample programme was presented to the planners for approval.

They turned it down. But more than that, they said that Archie would never be a strong enough character to sustain his own show.

The blow preyed on Brough's mind so much that it affected his health and led to a recurrence of an old chest complaint. Eventually in 1947 he was ordered to go to Switzerland for a cure.

In 1948 Brough returned, fully recovered and determined not to give up his radio ambitions. He persuaded the B.B.C. to give him a series featuring himself and Peter Cavanagh (the 'Voice of Them All') as the sole cast and, with Charles Maxwell as Producer, the new show *Two's a Crowd* took the air to become a modest success for all concerned.

Again when the radio series ended in late 1948, Archie and Brough went on a music-hall tour but now another piece of misfortune came their way. It had been impossible to persuade any theatrical management to book the act as a top-of-the-bill attraction and so Archie and Brough were in the supporting cast of a show headed by Turner Layton at the Glasgow Empire. One night, Val Parnell, who had been elected to the Board of Moss Empires in succession to George Black, walked in during the first house and found the theatre half empty. As a result, Brough didn't receive another engagement from the Moss Empires circuit for two years by which time *Educating Archie* was on the air.

The year 1949, however, marked the turn of the tide. Wally Ridley was by this time an executive with E.M.I. and a close friend of Donald Peers. It was at the request of Donald and Wally that Peter Brough and Archie Andrews turned up one Sunday night at the King's Theatre, Hammersmith, to do the 'warm-up' for the first programme of that phenomenal radio series. Afterwards, Peter talked to Roy Speer who produced *Cavalier of Song* and had been responsible for a Vera Lynn series. Speer was enthusiastic about an Archie Andrews show and persuaded Michael Standing, the Head of the Variety Department, to authorize another trial programme.

This time Brough hit on the idea of Archie's education. But obviously he would have to have a private tutor as the programme budget wouldn't run to an entire class of children. The choice fell on Robert Moreton, who was balanced by an odd-job man played by twenty-seven-year-old Max Bygraves. The fair sex was represented by Miss Hattie Jacques, who had made her radio name in *ITMA*.

Many friends turned up at the trial recording, among them Donald Peers, and the whole thing obviously went off very well, for a short time later Brough, who had prepared himself for another disappointment, was told that the show would be given a run of six weeks – with an option of a further six – in June of the following year, 1950.

On 6 June 1950, the first edition of *Educating Archie* went on the air and Donald Peers returned the compliment by doing the pre-broadcast warm-up for Archie and Brough. The new programme occupied the spot that had been previously filled by *Take It From Here*, a show which had won the *Daily Mail*'s National Radio Award in 1949 and it was no enviable task to step into the shoes of Dick Bentley, Joy Nichols, and Jimmy Edwards, but Archie acquitted himself very well.

*Hattie Jacques, Robert Moreton, Archie Andrews, and Peter Brough.*

Every national daily gave the programme glowing reviews. The famous Radio Critic, Collie Knox, summed it up when he wrote:

> Peter Brough in his *Educating Archie* fun and games is content to play Dummy, and give his famous 'Archie' most of the 'calls'. Wise in his generation, he has also co-opted two clever script-writers, Eric Sykes and Sid Colin, with alert support from Moreton and Bygraves. The result is so far a cosy, clean and rib-tickling show.

The B.B.C. was quick to take up its additional six-week option and eventually the programme, planned as a summer filler, ran for an unprecedented thirty consecutive weeks. By the end of that run its audience increased from four million to twelve, rivalling even award-winning *Take It From Here*, the show it was supposed to replace. And replace it, it did, for on 20 October 1950, *Educating Archie* was awarded the *Daily Mail*'s National Radio Award as the best programme of the year.

Suddenly Archie Andrews *and* Peter Brough were very much in demand. The theatre circuits wanted them as top-of-the-bill attractions – offers came in from Bernard Delfont, George Black, Tom Arnold, and Val Parnell. At the same time Harry Alan Towers wanted Archie to appear in his own show on Radio Luxemburg and offered a fee of £1,200 per programme which was vastly more than the B.B.C. was prepared to pay. But the Corporation responded by offering a three-year contract for *Educating Archie* and Brough accepted.

The extent of the commercial exploitation of the Archie Andrews phenomenon was remarkable. His face appeared on key-rings, jigsaw-puzzles, cut-out books, scarves, slippers, sweets, painting-books, and so on. His adventures were retold in annuals and life-size models of him were manufactured. When the Meddocream factory produced Archie Andrews lollipops they sold fifteen million in the first year and the Archie Andrews Club that they sponsored had 200,000 members. And, of course, there was Archie Andrews soap, made by Imperial Leather. And besides the commercial use of Archie, he also appeared in Road Safety and National Savings Campaigns and in publicity for the Infantile Paralysis Fund.

Meanwhile, the B.B.C. were anxious to use

their award-winning star but Archie – or rather Peter Brough – had to turn down their offer to resume the radio series in April 1951 because Eric Sykes, the programme's script-writer, was busy writing a series for Frankie Howerd. Brough was determined not to jeopardize the show by employing a new writer and so the programme was put back to the later part of the year.

When it did return on 3 August 1951, it was decided to make a change in the cast and Tony Hancock, who had recently established his name in *Variety Bandbox*, succeeded Robert Moreton as Archie's tutor. The rest of the cast stayed the same. The show had made stars of Moreton and Bygraves and it would soon do the same for Hancock, who took the whole thing very seriously and insisted that Archie should attend the script rehearsal and read his own lines.

*Tutor Hancock.*

The second series had only run for a few weeks when Max Bygraves was asked to star in a Broadway show with Judy Garland. Brough advised him to accept and set about looking for a replacement but it was no easy task. Max had established himself as the key comic of the programme with famous catch-phrases like 'That's a good idea, son' and 'I've arrived and to prove it – I'm here!'

At first Alfred Marks, then the resident comedian of the B.B.C.'s *Starlight Hour*, stepped in but was only able to stay for two weeks. Then Brough came up with, of all names, Gilbert Harding. To ask Gilbert to take on the role of handyman that Max had created and to deliver lines like 'Blimey, Archie, lad, and what have you bin a-doing of?' was expecting a lot, but to Brough's astonishment he agreed. In order to fit him into the plot, Gilbert was cast as Hancock's former Headmaster which gave him plenty of opportunity to vent his spleen on Tony and at the same time strike up a friendship with Archie. But as was the case with Alfred Marks, the B.B.C. thought that it wouldn't be in Gilbert's own interests to remain as a featured player in *Educating Archie* for long and so after a few weeks he too left the cast. For the rest of the run the show relied on guest artists until on the last programme of the series Max Bygraves arrived back.

Undoubtedly the star of the second series was Tony Hancock with his catch-phrase 'Flipping kids.' It made a star of him as it had of Robert

*Max Bygraves, one of the stars of* Educating Archie.

Moreton, Max Bygraves and would do for Beryl Reid and Harry Secombe, both of whom appeared in the third series. In 1952 it again won the *Daily Mail*'s National Radio Award and in 1953 Brough, for the third time in as many years had to once again turn down an extension to the run of the series because of the strain that it would place on its cast and on Eric Sykes, its script-writer. And in that year yet another famous name joined the cast – Bernard Miles as the tinker.

*Educating Archie* was an amazing show in many different ways. As I said at the beginning, its very existence as a radio programme was almost a contradiction because the whole point of ventriloquism is a visual illusion. It was also remarkable in the people who appeared in it. Besides Max Bygraves, Tony Hancock, Beryl Reid (Monica), Harry Secombe, Ronald Chesney, and the host of other people that it made, it also introduced thirteen-year-old Julie Andrews to the radio audience. And it was so amazingly popular. Besides all his other activities Brough became responsible for organizing the annual Royal Household Party at Windsor Castle, a duty he has enjoyed for many years, and Archie Andrews entertained the late King George VI and the present Royal Family on many occasions.

Archie Andrews was more than just a block of wood as became so obvious when he was 'kidnapped' in 1951. The person responsible anonymously sent a note saying that Archie could be found at the Lost Property Office at King's Cross Station but while he was missing, millions followed the case as if a real child had been lost. But then perhaps he was *too* real and like all real children he had to grow up for, in 1958, *Educating Archie* was broadcast for the last time.

Like so many of the early post-war shows, *Educating Archie* still remains puzzling. What was the secret of this ventriloquist's dummy or of the fictional Dick Barton; what made Wilfred Pickles the greatest broadcasting star in wireless history and why did those astonishing scenes take place during Donald Peers's 1949 series? Whatever the answer it had something to do with the astonishing power that radio had and that television lacks.

# 14. New Directions

When the 1950s began, television was regarded by everybody in 'the business', by which I mean show business and the entertainment industry generally, as a minority service. If you owned a set and lived in the Greater London Area (which was the only place where programmes could be received) then you could buy the special television edition of the *Radio Times*, which in 1950 gave the entire week's TV programmes on pages forty-six and forty-seven.

A glance at those programmes would show just how much of a poor relation the new medium was. Few major stars bothered to appear on it. It was regarded more as a training-ground for newcomers and even in the middle of the 1950s when reference books reviewed an artist's career they would state the occasion on which he or she had *broadcast*, by which they meant radio work, and then briefly add 'and has also televised'. Strangely enough many of the top radio shows of the early 1950s would probably have been more suitable for the new medium. Domestic comedies such as *Life With the Lyons* seemed to lend themselves to television but the attitude to it was similar to that displayed by many artists towards talking pictures before their introduction. Some big radio names had their own TV series; those of Donald Peers and Frankie Howerd both made their appearance in the same week of 1951 but it was, as I have said, a minority service which most people were content to leave alone.

It was in radio that the important things happened.

And in the early 1950s new ground certainly was being broken on the wireless especially in the field of comedy. One particularly excellent programme which began in 1953 was called *In All Directions* and starred Peter Ustinov and Peter Jones who together wrote the script and played all the parts. Jones as an East End spiv called Dudley, who transacted all his business in a telephone-kiosk, was a joy to listen to. It was an altogether more sophisticated type of humour than had been heard before.

Frankie Howerd was riding high too. *Variety Bandbox*, which he and Derek Roy hosted on alternate weeks, had made a star of him but his more satirical approach to humour was still a decade away in 1953.

He was just one of the huge number of young comics who were released from the Services in late 1946.

Among the others were Alfred Marks, Jimmy Edwards, Peter Sellers, Michael Bentine, Harry Secombe, Graham Stark, Morecambe and Wise, Harry Worth, who was then a ventriloquist, and Tony Hancock.

There was a great friendship between these comics and virtually any of them could have teamed up in those early days. At one time it seemed probable that Peter Sellers and Tony Hancock would have worked together. They spent their last months in the Services together looking after the costumes and props of the Army 'Gang' shows. They were allowed to wear civilian clothes and affected to be well-known show-

*Peter Ustinov and Peter Jones, the stars of* In All Directions, *1953.*

business figures, calling themselves Mr de Sellers and Mr le Hancock. Indeed it was Sellers who gave Hancock the inspiration for one of his famous routines, the Hunchback of Notre-Dame, when Tony saw Peter entertaining two W.A.A.F.s with his interpretation of Dr Jekyll and Mr Hyde.

Few people could have realized in 1945 that each of these two men would one day be regarded as a genius in the field of comedy.

Both their careers took a long time getting off the ground, and despite the enormous cult that came to surround *The Goon Show* towards the end of its life, Sellers was never in the same league as Hancock as far as broadcasting was concerned.

*The Goon Show* was first heard in 1951,

Variety Bandbox *star, Frankie Howerd in 1951.*

*Peter Sellers and Harry Secombe rehearsing at Grafton's Pub, Victoria, for the first edition of* Crazy People *which began in 1951. In the background is Michael Bentine (left) and Spike Milligan (right).*

*Milligan, Secombe, and Sellers, 1953.*

although it was then called *Crazy People*. At the time it was a rather secondary programme for Sellers and Secombe who were much better known for their respective roles in *Ray's a Laugh* and *Educating Archie* but for Michael Bentine and Terence Milligan, better known as Spike, it was their first major radio break.

It would be stupid to pretend that *The Goon Show* was a startling innovation in radio humour. Far from it. Surrealism in sound had become almost 'old hat' in B.B.C. comedy by 1950. It was something that the wireless could do very well as *Bandwagon* had shown before the war and *ITMA* had proved conclusively for a decade. And Elkan and Dorothean Allen in their excellent book *Good Listening* said this about a show which they considered to be 'in a class of its own':

> It attempts to reproduce in sound something of the Marx Brothers' madness. This is done by the use of extravagant situations, completely divorced from reality, and sheer lunatic characterization. Gas-filled women float like blimps along the ceiling, men bounce back ten storeys from the ground, and suchlike absurdities.

It was not, however, a reference to *The Goon Show* but a description of *Danger Men At Work* – a show which popped in and out of the programme schedules during the 1940s. Which all goes to show that the Goons were not in fact the inventors or even the pioneers of radio Surrealism. But then they never claimed to be. Later their enthusiastic followers would try to see *The Goon Show* as *the* great breakthrough in British humour.

In fact *The Goon Show* or *Crazy People* as it was, didn't make much of an impact in its early years. It only really became a cult after television had become the major medium of broadcasting.

Then in the mid and late 1950s a new generation of teenagers – an age group that had never previously seemed to exist – discovered Sellers, Secombe, and Milligan and made them their heroes.

This new audience knew nothing of *ITMA* and *Bandwagon*. They were hearing a programme that used the wireless medium to its full advantage for, what was to them, the very first time. Neddy, Bluebottle, Major Bloodnock, Moriarty, Henry Crun, Minny and the rest became what Funf and Chinstrap had been to their parents. And, of course, the humour was a little more advanced than it had been fifteen years before. What *The Goon Show* did, in fact, was to perfect the art of pure radio comedy at a time when radio itself was losing its audience to television. The programme travelled further down the Surrealist road than any other had done but it was a purely radio road that it travelled on. A couple of half-hearted attempts to produce Goon Shows on television ended in failure and the programme went off the air, together with so many other top B.B.C. shows, when the 1950s ended.

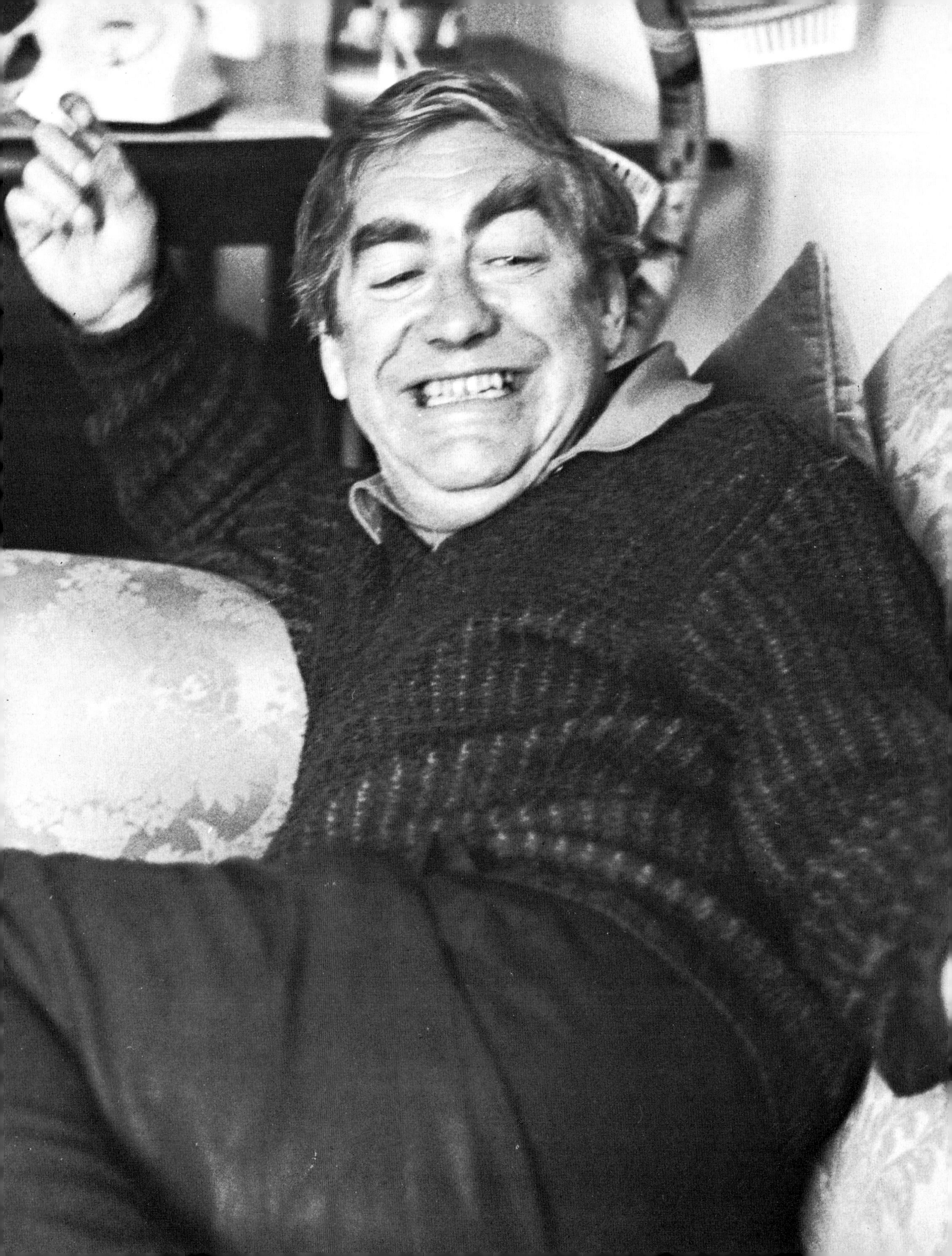

# 15. The Lad Himself

Tony Hancock is significant, from the point of view of this book, because he was the bridge between radio and television. He was the last great star to be created by the wireless. He went on to become the greatest television star of his time and when he died in 1968 his passing was mourned in the same way as Tommy Handley's had been almost two decades before.

He was born Anthony John Hancock on 12 May 1924 at Small Heath, Birmingham and when he was three years old the family moved to Bournemouth where his father took a hotel. Jack Hancock (Tony's father) was a semi-pro with many friends in the profession and among those who visited him at the Railway Hotel, Bournemouth were Clapham and Dwyer, Elsie and Doris Waters, the Houston Sisters and 'Stainless Stephen'. It was contact with these people that led Tony to think of the stage as a career.

He left Bradfield College when he was fifteen and his first job, at Hector Powe's, lasted exactly two hours and thirty-five minutes. He next became a Board of Trade civil servant and also made his first appearance as a comedian.

This was during the early days of the war and Tony, dressed like Max Miller and billed as 'Anthony Hancock . . . the Confidential Comic' earned a fee of ten shillings. Most of his early attempts at comedy were disastrous and after more jobs and a small spot in a B.B.C. half-hour, he was called up for the R.A.F. Regiment in 1942.

Once in the Forces, Hancock managed to get himself into the camp concert party and got an audition for E.N.S.A. But his nerve failed him after the words, 'Ladies and Gentlemen' and he dried up completely. He was more successful with Squadron Leader Ralph Reader who accepted him for one of his Army 'Gang' shows and Hancock together with such friends as Graham Stark happily spent the rest of the war in North Africa and Italy entertaining the troops.

On being released from the Services Hancock fell in with a group of gifted and out-of-work young comedians who found it cheaper to starve together and in those days Hancock lived on a diet of one sausage a day which he eked out with frequent glasses of water. Ironically, his first professional work as a civilian was in another Ralph Reader Gang Show called *Wings* which consisted of about 300 ex-R.A.F. men.

Inevitably Hancock eventually found his way on to the bill at the Windmill Theatre as half of a double act with a pianist called Derek Scott. The act consisted of impressions of a sea-side concert party – it was the sort of thing that Hancock could do very well, and did do, perhaps for longer than he should have done.

A great deal of his repertoire was developed in those immediate post-war days; much of it was based on the work of his father's friend, George Fairweather, a Bournemouth postman who had become a professional just before the war. Fairweather did impressions of people like George Arliss, the famous English actor who had gone to Hollywood and made a large number of films in which he had played such parts as Disraeli and Rothschild. Fairweather imitated him 'straight' and dropped him from his act when Arliss died in 1946 at the age of seventy-seven. Hancock, however, was still doing his deliberately hammed-up Arliss imitation twenty years later although he did introduce it with the words 'And now here's one for the teenagers.'

A B.B.C. audition introduced him to Denis Main Wilson who booked Tony for some *Workers' Playtime* broadcasts. Also at that audition was an agent called Phyllis Rounce. Under her management Hancock was to rise from earning £15 a week at the Windmill to £500 a week in the West End and when his contract with Miss Rounce came up for renewal Hancock would show his gratitude by telling the stage-door keeper that she was not to be allowed to see him. But that came much later.

The first thing Phyllis did was to get Tony a summer season engagement at Bognor Regis in a show run by B. C. Hilliam of 'Flotsam and Jetsam' fame. From the four acts that he provided for the show (Hilliam had actually asked for five), Hancock afterwards constructed *the* act – the one which was to become his standby for the next two decades. Charles Laughton, as the Hunchback of Notre-Dame and as Captain Bligh of the *Bounty*, was in it; so was Robert Newton as Long John Silver and, of course, George Arliss and, best of all, the Gaumont-British montage in which Hancock played the town-crier, the athletes, and the diving swimmer.

But things were still very bleak for Hancock and his fellow comedians. With Harry Secombe, he picked up a week's work in an out-of-season show at Blackpool; and with Larry Stevens, who was to write *The Goon Show* with Spike Milligan, he ran a wildly unsuccessful and illegal book-making business from a succession of basement flats. And he did a spot in pantomime which had Julie Andrews as Principal Girl. His part was Jolly Jenkins – and he hated it.

*Tony with Frankie Howerd in* Variety Bandbox.

During this time Hancock made his début on television but after a couple of appearances he decided that it wasn't for him. Then he appeared on *Variety Bandbox*, the show that had made overnight stars of Derek Roy, Frankie Howerd, and Arthur English. He was a disaster and the Producer told Phyllis Rounce never to bring 'that man' near him again. But she did and within a few months Hancock was appearing quite regularly.

The year 1951 was the one that made Hancock a star. Derek Roy now had an hour-long show called *Happy Go Lucky* which included a regular sketch about a Scout patrol. Hancock was the Scoutmaster. His Scouts were Peter Butterworth, Bill Kerr and, an old friend, Graham Stark, who was in the show on Hancock's recommendation. Tony was much relieved when new script-writers were brought in and the Scout sketch was dropped. The new writers were introduced to Denis Main Wilson by Gale Pedrick; their names were Ray Galton and Alan Simpson and they had met in a sanatorium in the Isle of Wight. Hancock liked their material and asked them to write for him for half of his fee, thus trebling what they had previously been paid.

Meanwhile Hancock, in 1951, succeeded Robert Moreton as tutor to Archie Andrews and overnight became a top radio name. As Clifford Davis, the Radio Critic of the *Daily Mirror* said: 'Tony (Flippin' Kids) Hancock shoots to star billing in his first outing with the Archie team. This man is funny . . . Verdict: Flippin' fine.'

'Tony (Flippin' Kids) Hancock' wasn't, however, the way in which he wanted to be billed. He always had a dislike of catch-phrases, gimmicks, and funny voices despite the fact that he often resorted to them himself. None the less the phrase 'Flippin Kids' made him a star and he got on well with *Educating Archie*'s script-writer, Eric Sykes. And suddenly he found himself in demand. He appeared at the Prince of Wales Theatre in *Archie Andrews' Christmas Party* at 11 a.m. and 2.30 p.m. and at 6.15 and 8.30 p.m. he was in the cast of a Val Parnell revue at the same theatre. And Phyllis Rounce was getting him Sunday concert engagements at 200 guineas a time.

In 1952 he opened in Jack Hylton's show *London Laughs* at the Adelphi co-starring with Vera Lynn and Jimmy Edwards. He replaced Dick Bentley who had left the show before it opened, after a disagreement over billing, and despite the vast differences between Hancock's style and that of Edwards', the two comedians worked happily and well together. In November he appeared in the Royal Variety Show with Ted Ray, Gracie Fields, Bud Flanagan, and Gigli. He was a great success. At the time, Dennis Main Wilson was producing a radio show which had begun life as *Forces All Star Bill*. By this time it had been abbreviated to *All Star Bill* and would later be just *Star Bill*. Later still it would become *Hancock's Half Hour*. The programme, which was written by Galton and Simpson and included Graham Stark in the cast, had adopted the practice of having a different guest-star comedian every week, but now Main Wilson decided to get a resident comic and his choice fell on Tony Hancock. Back at the Adelphi Hancock began to show the first signs of strain. He was already drinking fairly heavily but not enough to affect his actual performance on stage and the ordeal, as Hancock found it, of doing the same show night after night was proving to be too much, so Hylton agreed to allow Tony to take a few weeks' holiday with his wife Cicely.

When he returned he was signed up for another Hylton show at Blackpool which would later be transferred to the Adelphi under the title *Talk of the Town*. After a few weeks he tried to get out of the summer show claiming that the strain was affecting his health. He even produced a note to this effect from a Bolton psychiatrist. Jack Hylton, himself a Bolton man, was unimpressed and Hancock remained in the show.

On radio, *All Star Bill* had, significantly, been shortened to *Star Bill* and one day Graham Stark, who had been in the show since it began, got a message to go and see Dennis Main Wilson who told him that there were going to be only six more shows in the then present series which

had been running for two years. Hancock had already told Stark that they were going to have a rest for a few weeks but Main Wilson said that there would be certain 'policy changes', which Stark knew meant only one thing – he was being dropped from the show. Eventually Main Wilson admitted that Tony himself was recasting the show and that it was going to be called *Hancock's Half Hour*. About the same time Tony had Phyllis Rounce barred from his dressing-room. Her contract had expired and he had signed with a new agent, Jack Adams of Kavanagh Associates.

The first edition of *Hancock's Half Hour* went out on 2 November 1954 and was heard by 12 per cent of the adult population as compared to the 25 per cent who had listened to *The Al Read Show* at the same time the previous week. Of those who did hear it, the opinion was that the script didn't do justice to its star. Moira Lister appeared in a few of the early programmes as Hancock's girl-friend but later Hattie Jacques became the only regular female star in the show. Patricia Hayes, however, did appear sporadically as Mrs Cravat. And the other regulars were there from the beginning, Sid James, Bill Kerr, and Kenneth Williams.

The day before the second series began, Hancock fled to France for no apparent reason and for the first four programmes Robin Boyle had to announce 'This is the B.B.C. Light Programme. We present *Hancock's Half Hour* starring Harry Secombe, Sidney James, Bill Kerr . . .'. Hancock eventually returned and no explanation was asked for or given. Only Hancock could have got away with it.

By this time the scripts had greatly improved and by early 1955 the show had established itself and its star as a major development in British comedy and Anthony Aloysius St John Hancock of 23 Railway Cuttings, East Cheam, became one of the best-loved comic inventions of broadcasting. Like Anthony John Hancock the actor, the fictional character with his homburg hat and the astrakhan collar had many apparently unpleasant attributes. The Hancock of East Cheam was pompous, arrogant, childish, petty, and ignorant but that didn't stop anyone from liking him. The real Hancock was equally pompous in a different sort of way and he could be callous and unkind in a way that the fictional Hancock could never be, but that didn't stop people from loving him. When in 1956 *Hancock's Half Hour* transferred to B.B.C. Television, Bill Kerr was dropped from the cast. After a series of arguments between Hancock and Galton and Simpson about using Kenneth Williams's 'snide' voice, he too left after the sixth show of the series and Hattie Jacques was only used occasionally. Eventually even Sid James had to go. Hancock could survive all this. He was right when he said that he didn't need to be part of a double act or to use 'funny voices' to get laughs. Some of the great classics of the television series featured Hancock either totally alone or with character actors.

The split with Galton and Simpson was a different matter however. They had created the Hancock that the public knew and loved. Perhaps if the public knew the real Hancock well enough they might have loved him too as so many people did but that was not possible.

The later story of Tony Hancock is still fresh in the minds of most people and it does not belong to the story of radio anyway. And the history of Hancock's private life – his two marriages, his heavy drinking, and his frequent quarrels with associates is now common knowledge. And yet none of it seems to detract from the lovableness of Tony Hancock. When he killed himself in Australia in 1968 the sense of loss to his public was a personal one as no other's had been except Tommy Handley's. The post-war generation had lost the greatest comic genius of its time.

But in 1955 that was a long way off. Then Hancock was still surrounded by Sid James, Bill Kerr, Kenneth Williams, and Hattie Jacques. He was still saying 'stone me' and 'you buffoon!' and getting his quotations mixed up. And more than anything else he was making us laugh at ourselves and at realistic everyday situations. The boring Sunday afternoon was a classic. So was the reunion when nobody had anything to say to one another.

Hancock was the symbol of his times; the link between the old cosy world of the wireless and the new realistic, and perhaps more mundane, world of television. For some time his radio programme ran concurrently with his television show. But by 1956 when the first TV *Hancock's Half Hour* was transmitted the wireless, as we knew it, was dead and Hancock had been its last star.

# 16. Postscript

On the evening of Thursday 22 September 1955, British Independent Television transmitted its first programmes which were produced by Associated Rediffusion and the Associated Broadcasting Company. The first advertised event was at seven-fifteen when the guests arrived for the Gala Ceremony at the Guildhall, London to hear speeches from the Postmaster-General, Dr Charles Hill, and the Chairman of the Independent Television Authority, Sir Kenneth Clark. The ceremony was followed by a show simply called *Variety*, introduced by Jack Jackson. Among those taking part were Shirley Abicair, Billy Cotton, Leslie Welch, Reg Dixon, Derek Roy, John Hanson, Harry Secombe and two men whose shows began on I.T.V. that week – Michael Miles and Hughie Green.

*Take Your Pick* complete with the 'Yes No Interlude' and *Double Your Money* with its thousand pound treasure trail and *Sunday Night At The London Palladium* all made their debut that week. Other attractions included Dame Edith Evans as Lady (A Handbag!) Bracknell, Lucille Ball in *I Love Lucy*, *The Adventures of Noddy*, Richard Greene in *Robin Hood*, and Dr Billy Graham.

Despite this magnificent line-up, it was a radio story that captured the newspaper headlines the next morning for at six forty-five, a few minutes before I.T.V. went on the air, the B.B.C. 'killed' Grace Archer the fictional wife of 'young master Phil Archer' in the 'everyday story of country folk'. Although they recently admitted the truth, at the time B.B.C. officials claimed that the timing of this dramatic episode was entirely coincidental.

The Corporation was equally disingenuous about its new plans for an improved television service which were announced in the same week. The B.B.C. managed to devote several pages of the *Radio Times* to this subject without once referring to the existence of its rival. But despite its clever ploy with Grace Archer and the huge fuss that it made over the Silver Wedding of Wilfred and Mabel Pickles, which occurred in the same week, the B.B.C. knew that Television was now the major medium of broadcasting and that an era had come to an end.

And that really is the end of the book – but not quite. As they used to say when a radio show under-ran its time; 'We find that we have a little time in hand before the start of the next programme so here are some gramophone records' – or in this case photographs, on the following pages, of some more of those wonderful Wireless Stars.

*Layton and Johnstone were one of the most popular singing duets of the twenties and thirties but Johnstone's career never recovered from the scandal when he was cited in the divorce action that Albert Sandler, the famous violinist, brought against his wife. Turner Layton (left) however remained a top of the bill star for many years.*

Opposite, left: *A wartime photograph of Mr Cyril Fletcher broadcasting. His first 'Odd Ode' was heard before the War.*
Opposite, right: *Brian Reece as P.C. 49, seen here with his fiancée Joan, played by Joy Shelton. The adventures of Archibald Berkeley Willoughby (P.C. 49) began in October 1946.*

94C P

Above: *'Young Eamonn Andrews of Dublin' as he was billed in the* Radio Times, *made his B.B.C. debut as Question-Master of* Ignorance Is Bliss *– a 'brainless Brains Trust' starring (left to right) Harold Berens, Gladys Hay, and Michael Moore.*

Opposite, left: *Arthur English, star of* Variety Bandbox *reached the top by portraying the typical 'spiv' so prevalent in the post-war era.*
Opposite, right: *Ronnie Ronalde was in sharp contrast to the 'spiv' image of Arthur English. Ronnie's youth and his great ability as a yodeller and whistler endeared him to millions of post-war housewives.*

BBC

BBC

Above: *Elsie and Doris Waters were seldom off the airwaves in the forties. Chiefly famous for their portrayal of 'Gert and Daisy' they are seen here with their equally popular brother, Jack Warner.*

Opposite: *'Only A Rose' was the signature tune of husband and wife team Anne Ziegler and Webster Booth without whose duets no wireless variety bill was ever really complete.*

Above: *Jimmy Jewell and Ben Warris starred in a number of successful radio series. In this picture they are seen with Harold Berens and Eric Phillips playing 'Luigi' and the 'Dude' respectively.*

Opposite: *Still going strong, Dickie Murdoch and Arthur Askey – almost one could say, the men who started it all.*

# Index

Figures in italics indicate a page with a photograph of the subject.